T0129218

GOD
IS WELL PLEASED WITH
YOU

TERESA GOREE

WESTBOW
PRESS®
A DIVISION OF THOMAS NELSON
& ZONDERVAN

Copyright © 2017 Teresa Goree.

All rights reserved. No part of this book may be used or reproduced by
any means, graphic, electronic, or mechanical, including photocopying,
recording, taping or by any information storage retrieval system
without the written permission of the author except in the case of
brief quotations embodied in critical articles and reviews.

This book is a work of non-fiction. Unless otherwise noted, the author
and the publisher make no explicit guarantees as to the accuracy of
the information contained in this book and in some cases, names of
people and places have been altered to protect their privacy.

WestBow Press books may be ordered through booksellers or by contacting:

WestBow Press
A Division of Thomas Nelson & Zondervan
1663 Liberty Drive
Bloomington, IN 47403
www.westbowpress.com
1 (866) 928-1240

Because of the dynamic nature of the Internet, any web addresses or
links contained in this book may have changed since publication and
may no longer be valid. The views expressed in this work are solely those
of the author and do not necessarily reflect the views of the publisher,
and the publisher hereby disclaims any responsibility for them.

Any people depicted in stock imagery provided by Thinkstock are models,
and such images are being used for illustrative purposes only.
Certain stock imagery © Thinkstock.

ISBN: 978-1-5127-8828-0 (sc)
ISBN: 978-1-5127-8830-3 (hc)
ISBN: 978-1-5127-8829-7 (e)

Library of Congress Control Number: 2017907950

Print information available on the last page.

WestBow Press rev. date: 05/23/2017

Scripture quotations taken from the Amplified® Bible (AMPC),
Copyright © 1954, 1958, 1962, 1964, 1965, 1987 by The Lockman Foundation
Used by permission. www.Lockman.org

Scripture taken from the King James Version of the Bible.

Scripture taken from the New King James Version®. Copyright © 1982
by Thomas Nelson. Used by permission. All rights reserved.

The Holy Bible, English Standard Version® (ESV®) Copyright © 2001 by
Crossway, a publishing ministry of Good News Publishers. All rights reserved.
ESV® Text Edition: 2016

Scripture quotations marked (GNT) are from the Good News
Translation in Today's English Version- Second Edition Copyright
© 1992 by American Bible Society. Used by Permission.

Scriptures taken from the Holy Bible, New International Version®, NIV®.
Copyright © 1973, 1978, 1984, 2011 by Biblica, Inc.™ Used by permission
of Zondervan. All rights reserved worldwide. www.zondervan.com The
"NIV" and "New International Version" are trademarks registered in
the United States Patent and Trademark Office by Biblica, Inc.™

Scripture quotations are taken from the Holy Bible, New Living
Translation, copyright ©1996, 2004, 2007, 2013, 2015 by Tyndale
House Foundation. Used by permission of Tyndale House Publishers,
Inc., Carol Stream, Illinois 60188. All rights reserved.

Scripture quotations taken from the New American Standard Bible® (NASB),
Copyright © 1960, 1962, 1963, 1968, 1971, 1972, 1973,
1975, 1977, 1995 by The Lockman Foundation
Used by permission. www.Lockman.org"

Scripture marked "Darby" taken from the Darby Translation of the Bible.

Scripture taken from the Wycliffe Bible (WYC) 2001 by Terence P. Noble.

Scripture marked "YLT" from the Young's Literal Translation of the Bible.

CONTENTS

Author's Note..ix

Acknowledgements..xi

Introduction..xiii

Creation and Man...1

Perception Changes...7

Glory and Honor Given to Christ 13

Glory and Honor Given to Man.....................................24

Righteousness Revealed..34

A New Creation 42

Glory Within 44

Glory to Another..50

Receiving the Word..55

We Live What We Believe...67

A New Perspective in Christ...80

God Is Good...92

Intimacy..95

God Is Love 102

We've Been Honored and Glorified..............................107

AUTHOR'S NOTE

For the purpose of bringing the most accurate meaning to the scriptures used in this book, I have presented a variety of Bible translations for the same verse. Using multiple versions of the Bible can help to expand and clarify the intended meaning for the reader. This approach is made for the purpose of allowing the reader to have a better understanding of the scripture in its entirety. The Bible was originally written in the languages of Hebrew, Aramaic and Greek. So by providing several translations, the reader is given a broader and more precise insight of the original words and meanings.

ACKNOWLEDGEMENTS

I want to thank my family; Dad, Mom, Marshon and Brad who have always loved, supported and encouraged me along every step of this life's journey. I love and appreciate you so much!

To my children, Justin, Sara, Jeremiah and Emily who have always been my greatest and most cherished blessing. Thank you for all your pep talks!

To my dear friend Phyllis, my prayer partner, whose inspiration has always lifted me, thank you!

To my dear friend, Mariane, whose faith in our amazing God has so blessed me, thank you!

INTRODUCTION

I believe there is one aspect to a person's life that all people would agree they desire. I believe that aspect is the desire to be a valued individual. This is an inherited quality that every human being is born with. For a person to know his or her life has value, he or she must have a sense of acceptance and dignity as a human being. These qualities serve to establish that each individual life matters and has significance and purpose.

There is only one source from which people can receive their value at the level that brings complete and total fulfillment. God the Father is that source. The purpose for writing this book is to explain this truth as the Lord explained and unfolded it to me. It is my hope and prayer that you will open your heart and receive the truth of this word.

To have the highest value that only God can impart to our identity, we must have the correct and complete perspective. How we perceive our life affects every aspect of it. Perspective is defined as the faculty of seeing all the relevant data in a meaningful relationship. Our perspective is our viewpoint. It is our approach, our direction, and our attitude. Our perspective is our demeanor, our bent, our inclination. It is our vision, our mind-set, and our belief system. Our perspective affects every part of our life. It affects how our character develops, how we interact with others, and most importantly, our relationship with God. If our perspective is correct, clear, and unhindered, we will see and experience life in its fullness and receive our true identity as valued human beings. However, if our perspective is obscured, dim, or unclear, we will see and experience life with limitations.

CREATION AND MAN

In Genesis 1 we read how God Almighty, Creator of heaven and earth, spoke everything we see into existence. Hebrews 11:3 explains that the worlds were fashioned and put in order for their intended purpose by the Word of God, so that what we see was not made out of things that are visible. Genesis 1:1–31 (AMP) gives us the detailed account of this.

> In the beginning God (prepared, formed, fashioned, and) created the heavens and the earth. The earth was without form and an empty waste, and darkness was upon the face of the very great deep. The Spirit of God was moving (hovering, brooding) over the face of the waters. And God said, Let there be light; and there was light. And God saw that the light was good (suitable, pleasant) and He approved it; and God separated the light from the darkness. And God called the light Day, and the darkness He called Night. And there was evening and there was morning, one day. And God said, Let there be a firmament [the expanse of the sky] in the midst of the waters, and let it separate the waters [below] from the waters [above]. And God made the firmament [the expanse] and separated the waters which were under the expanse from the waters which were

above the expanse. And it was so. And God called the firmament Heavens. And there was evening and there was morning, a second day. And God said, Let the waters under the heavens be collected into one place [of standing], and let the dry land appear. And it was so. God called the dry land Earth, and the accumulated waters He called Seas. And God saw that this was good (fitting, admirable) and He approved it. And God said, Let the earth put forth [tender] vegetation: plants yielding seed and fruit trees yielding fruit whose seed is in itself, each according to its kind, upon the earth. And it was so. The earth brought forth vegetation: plants yielding seed according to their own kinds and trees bearing fruit in which was their seed, each according to its kind. And God saw that it was good (suitable, admirable) and He approved it. And there was evening and there was morning, a third day. And God said, Let there be lights in the expanse of the heavens to separate the day from the night, and let them be signs and tokens [of God's provident care], and [to mark] seasons, days, and years, And let them be lights in the expanse of the sky to give light upon the earth. And it was so. And God made the two great lights—the greater light (the sun) to rule the day and the lesser light (the moon) to rule the night. He also made the stars. And God set them in the expanse of the heavens to give light upon the earth, To rule over the day and over the night, and to separate the light from the darkness. And God saw that it was good (fitting, pleasant) and He approved it. And there was evening and there was morning, a fourth day. And God said, Let the waters bring forth abundantly and swarm with living creatures, and let birds fly over the earth in the open expanse of the heavens. God created the great sea monsters and every living creature that moves, which the waters brought forth abundantly, according to their kinds, and every winged bird according to its kind. And God saw that it was good (suitable, admirable) and He approved it. And God blessed them, saying, Be fruitful, multiply, and fill the waters in the seas, and let the fowl multiply in the earth. And there was evening and there was morning, a fifth day. And God said, Let the earth bring forth living creatures according to their kinds: livestock, creeping things, and [wild] beasts of the earth according to their kinds. And it was so. And God made the [wild] beasts of the earth according to their kinds, and domestic animals according to their kinds, and everything that creeps upon the earth according to its kind. And God saw that it was good (fitting, pleasant) and He approved it. God said, Let Us [Father, Son, and Holy Spirit] make mankind in Our image, after Our likeness, and let them have complete authority over the fish of the sea, the birds of the air, the [tame] beasts, and over all of the earth, and over everything that creeps upon the earth. So God created man in His own image, in the image and likeness of God He created him; male and female He created them. And God blessed them and said to them, Be fruitful, multiply, and fill the earth, and subdue it [using all its vast resources in the service of God and man]; and have dominion over the fish of the sea, the birds of the air, and over every living creature that moves upon the earth. And God said, See, I have given you every plant yielding seed that is on the face of all the land

3

and every tree with seed in its fruit; you shall have them for food. And to all the animals on the earth and to every bird of the air and to everything that creeps on the ground—to everything in which there is the breath of life—I have given every green plant for food. And it was so. And God saw everything that He had made, and behold, it was very good (suitable, pleasant) and He approved it completely. And there was evening and there was morning, a sixth day.

Notice that each time God created something by speaking, He then saw that it was good, and He approved it. Finally, on the last day, the sixth day, when He was finished with the creation of the heavens, the fullness of all the earth, and His most precious creation of all, man, He didn't just see that it was good and approve it, but He saw that it was very good, and He approved it completely!

So God the Creator spoke heaven and earth and all the host of them into existence. It was an amazingly beautiful and perfect creation for man and for life. Every minute detail, every exact measurement, every perfect calculation was gloriously fashioned and put in order by the wisdom of God for the existence of life. And God expressed His satisfaction with the magnificence of His creation. The Bible then goes on to say that God planted a garden toward the east, in Eden. The name Eden means "delight," and this is where God chose to place man. And God provided for man's needs and desires in all that He had created.

From the very beginning, we see the heart of our Creator. His passion is so wonderfully evident. The Bible says in Genesis 1:1–2 that as God prepared to create, His Spirit hovered over the face of the waters. This hovering means "to brood over, to weigh, to ponder, to consider closely." In the infinite mind of God, His plan and purpose for everything He had created was being set into motion, and the end result was astounding. Then He breathed the spirit of life into the man, Adam, and he became a living being placed in the midst of the beautiful creation in a place God called delight. Delight filled God's heart. Delight was His passion for us to experience. The wonder of His creation was to be our delight. Not only were we to enjoy the marvel and beauty of creation, but more importantly, we were to experience it in close union and intimacy with our Creator.

> The Lord God planted a garden toward the east, in Eden; and there He placed the man whom He had formed. Out of the ground the Lord God caused to grow every tree that is pleasing to the sight and good for food; the tree of life also in the midst of the garden, and the tree of the knowledge of good and evil. (Genesis 2:8–9 NASB)

The Bible goes on to tell us that God walked in this garden with the first man, Adam, in the cool of the day. They shared an intimate relationship, the Creator and His creation, in this place called delight. The word *delight* means "something that gives extreme pleasure." What a beautiful picture we see of the nature of God and His purpose for creating mankind. They walked together and talked with one another, communing and enjoying a close and intimate fellowship, delighting in one another. Oh, the heart of God is so evident and has not changed. Since the beginning, God planned and purposed to have a close relationship with man because it was His heart's intention and passionate desire and delight—the Creator and His created beings, sons and daughters, enjoying His creation with Him.

We also discover that Adam and Eve experienced an extraordinary freedom in this place of delight: "And the man and his wife were both naked and were not embarrassed or ashamed in each other's presence" (Genesis 2:25 AMP). "Now the man and his wife were both naked, but they felt no shame" (Genesis 2:25 NLT).

Although Adam and Eve were naked, they were comfortable in each other's presence; they were free in their minds, in their emotions, and in their bodies. They did not experience any shame, fear, embarrassment, inadequacy, or inferiority. They had no sense of weakness or deficiency. They were completely secure within themselves, with each other, and most importantly, in their relationship with God. They did not experience any sense of lack in their minds, in their emotions, or in their physical bodies. There were no questions or doubts about who they were. There were no questions or doubts about their relationship with God. They were in every respect completely free and completely whole. Their perception was correct. It was perfection. It was a perfect environment and a perfect relationship between God and man.

PERCEPTION CHANGES

Now when God put Adam in the Garden of Eden, he was given instructions to tend it, guard it, and keep it. God also told Adam what to eat and what not to eat—or we could say what to partake of in the garden and what not to partake of in the garden.

> And the Lord God commanded the man, saying, "Of every tree of the garden you may freely eat; but of the tree of the knowledge of good and evil you shall not eat, for in the day that you eat of it you shall surely die." (Genesis 2:16–17 NKJV)

Again we discover the heart of God toward man. He told Adam that he could freely eat of every tree but one. When you consider the enormity of this garden and all it contained, surely you would think that being told to eat from all except one tree would be easy. Now because of God's great love, He created man with the power to choose. It's called free will, and everyone born is given this wonderful privilege. We make our own choices. It's a gift from our Creator. He doesn't force us to do anything. That would go against who He is. God is love, and love gives. It never demands.

But one day the privilege of Adam's free will was put to the test by Satan, the serpent, whom the Bible describes as being more subtle, craftier, and more cunning than any living creature. He has no power except to deceive, and that is exactly what he did. As most people know, believers and unbelievers alike, Adam and Eve fell for his deception and ate from the tree of knowledge of good and evil that God told Adam not to eat from.

> Now the serpent was more cunning than any beast of the field which the Lord God had made. And he said to the woman, "Has God indeed said, 'You shall not eat of every tree of the garden'?" And the woman said to the serpent, "We may eat the fruit of the trees of the garden; but of the fruit of the tree which is in the midst of the garden, God has said, 'You shall not eat it, nor shall you touch it, lest you die.'" Then the serpent said to the woman, "You will not surely die. For God knows that in the day you eat of it your eyes will be opened, and you will be like God, knowing good and evil." So when the woman saw that the tree was good for food, that it was pleasant to the eyes, and a tree desirable to make one wise, she took of its fruit and ate. She also gave to her husband with her, and he ate. Then the eyes of both of them were opened, and they knew that they were naked; and they sewed fig leaves together and made themselves coverings. (Genesis 3:1–7 NKJV)

At this point, *everything* changed. Every aspect of God's creation was affected. The Bible says that as soon as they ate the fruit, they knew they were naked. Now that's interesting because we know Adam and Eve were naked before they ate the fruit, as we just read in Genesis 2:25. However, something had to change because now they recognized and acknowledged their nakedness so much so that they felt they needed to cover themselves. They did not recognize or have an understanding of their nakedness as being something that needed covering before they ate the fruit. The only explanation is that they did have a covering before they ate the fruit. It wasn't the type of covering like clothes that we would think of having today. They were covered in the glory, the honor, and the presence of God Himself! It was an actual covering they experienced and carried. It clothed them. It was glory upon them. It was honor that covered them. It was the presence of their Creator that clothed them. God said they were created in His image. He is light! He is love! He is glorious, radiant, and majestic. There was a brilliant and glorious splendor that covered their bodies. That is why Adam and Eve did not realize they were naked before they ate of the fruit from the tree of the knowledge of good and evil. The glory that God had given them covered their nakedness.

Now this glory, this honor, this presence that covered Adam and Eve was not only to clothe them, but it was much more than that. Their glorious covering gave them an appropriate view of the life God had given them. It was an accurate way of looking at themselves and their life. It was the viewpoint of God Himself. We can say that Adam and Eve were seeing through God's eyes. Remember, we just read that each time God created something, He *saw* that it was good, and He approved it! Their eyes saw the way God saw. They were seeing correctly because they were seeing God's perspective. They were seeing the way God sees.

However, when Adam and Eve ate the fruit, their eyes were opened to a different reality. Their viewpoint changed. Their entire perspective changed. Their perception of life as they had always known it suddenly changed. And because their perspective changed, they began to experience emotions they had never experienced before, as we find in the following verses.

> They heard the sound of the Lord God walking
> in the garden in the cool of the day, and the man

> and his wife hid themselves from the presence of
> the Lord God among the trees of the garden. Then
> the Lord God called to the man, and said to him,
> "Where are you?" He said, "I heard the sound of
> You in the garden, and I was afraid because I was
> naked; so I hid myself." And He said, "Who told
> you that you were naked? Have you eaten from
> the tree of which I commanded you not to eat?"
> (Genesis 3:8–11 NASB)

Here we find the Lord God walking in the garden as He had many
times before. However, this time what had always been a welcoming
sound to Adam and Eve actually provoked a feeling of dread so much
so that they hid from God. Notice that Adam said he was afraid
because he was naked. His reason for being fearful was because he
recognized that he was uncovered. He recognized that his covering
was gone. As a result, for the first time, Adam and Eve experienced
feelings of fear, embarrassment, and shame. They had no knowledge
of these emotions before eating the fruit. The consequence of these
feelings caused Adam to all of a sudden hide from his Creator, whom
he had walked with in perfect fellowship and harmony all his life.

I can't help but think that even though an infinite, omniscient Being
knew this would happen, there still had to be such a feeling of loss
in the beautiful relationship with His creation.

> God said, "Who told you that you were naked?
> Have you eaten of the tree of which I commanded
> you that you should not eat?" (Genesis 3:11 NASB)

At this point, God asked two very profound questions. He asked
Adam, "Who are you listening to, and which tree are you eating
from?" Of course, God knew the answer to these questions, but He
wanted Adam to consider the source of his fear and shame. Adam

had never known these emotions within himself. He had never experienced being afraid of anything, let alone being afraid of his Creator. Adam had only known the feelings of love and peace and joy that he shared with his God.

Remember, we just read how God created the heavens and the earth and all the host of them, and on the sixth day man was created.

> Then God said, "Let us make human beings in our image, to be like us. (NLT)

> Then God said, "And now we will make human beings; they will be like us and resemble us. (GNT)

So when Adam was created, the Bible says he was made in the image of the Father and of the Son and of the Holy Spirit. He was like God. The word *image* can be defined as representation, picture, or reflection! Adam was a reflection of his Creator. God created man to be like Him.

On the other hand, Satan said that if Adam and Eve were to eat the fruit from the tree of the knowledge of good and evil, their eyes would be opened and they would be like God. Here we find the first lie from the father of lies. As Jesus described him in the gospel of John:

> He was a murderer from the beginning and does not stand in the truth, because there is no truth in him. When he speaks a falsehood, he speaks what is natural to him, for he is a liar and the father of lies and of all that is false. (John 8:44 AMPC)

Adam and Eve were made in the image of God, made in His likeness. They were already like God. Did you hear that? They were already like God. It wasn't until they ate the fruit that they lost sight of the truth of who they were. They lost their perspective. The eyes of their understanding changed. The understanding of their identity changed. The perspective of who they were changed. Remember that after God said, "Let Us make man in Our image," He saw them and everything He had created, and it was very good and He approved it completely. They didn't need to change anything. There were no improvements needed. They were complete and perfect. They were like God. By eating the fruit of the knowledge of good and evil, however, they saw themselves in a different way. They saw themselves in a different light. They did not see themselves the way God saw them. They did not see themselves in the way they had been created. They did not see themselves as being made in the image and likeness of God. Their whole perspective changed, and they saw themselves, each other, and their Creator in a different light. The light had been replaced with darkness. They were in darkness, and they saw themselves in darkness. The truth was replaced with a lie, a false perception, and a false identity. The glory and honor that covered them were replaced with feelings of fear and shame. It was a complete reversal of God's original intent for man. The devil, Satan, deceived them. It was the lie of all lies. Adam was created in the image of God, but he no longer saw himself in that truth.

The glory and honor of man was lost.

GLORY AND HONOR
GIVEN TO CHRIST

W e know God had a plan. Of course He had a plan. The mind of God is unfathomable, unmeasurable, and unlimited. I once heard the mind of God described as a chess board made of forty-three levels. No matter what the situation is, God *always* has a solution. He's the Creator! It's amazing to realize that God knew exactly what Adam and Eve would do because in the mind of God, a wonderful plan was already in place. We read in Revelation 13 that Jesus was slain before the foundation of the world.

Nearly everyone knows the most-quoted verse in the Bible. We've seen it draped over stadium bleachers, plastered in huge bold letters on billboards, and beautifully written on bookmarks in every Christian bookstore. John 3:16 was God's plan to reconcile His relationship back to man, which Adam had forfeited through deception.

God's plan was to have an ongoing loving relationship with mankind. And just as in any truly loving relationship, it must be based on trust. The love between two people must have a foundation of trust. Similarly, it was necessary for man to trust in the goodness of his Creator, in order to experience and enjoy life in the fullness God intended. Adam needed to depend on the truth that God had his best interest at heart. Dependency requires complete and unwavering trust. Adam needed to identify with God his Creator as the source for all that was necessary to live his life in complete fulfillment. God had to be Adam's source for life.

So as John 3:16 tells us, God sent His Son to buy back the loving relationship Adam had lost.

> For God so loved the world that he gave his one and only Son, that whoever believes in him shall not perish but have eternal life. (John 3:16 NKJV)

We know from John 17:3 that eternal life is to know God and Jesus Christ His Son.

> And this is life eternal, that they might know thee the only true God, and Jesus Christ, whom thou hast sent. (John 17:3 KJV)

So we can interrupt John 3:16 as saying that God loved mankind so much that He gave Himself as a sacrifice in order that man would not be lost or have a false perspective of knowing who God was. Jesus came to show us the Father and the relationship He shared with God as a Son. Their relationship was exactly what God had intended for Adam.

Now for Jesus to redeem mankind, He had to represent Himself as a man before God, so He was born of flesh and blood through the virgin birth. This was necessary because death in the physical body had to be conquered. Remember, God told Adam that if he ate from the tree of the knowledge of good and evil, he would die. God's original intent was that man would always live in a body of optimum health and wholeness. It was never God's plan for man to die. Now we know that when Adam and Eve ate of the fruit, physical death did not happen immediately. However, the process of death began to work in their mortal bodies that had once been immortal. Many times when the Bible speaks about death, it is not just referring to physical death but the total cessation of life processes that eventually occur in all living organisms. The fall of Adam set into motion a deterioration process that took place on many levels, physically, mentally, and emotionally. It was an irreversible deterioration process. The key word here is *process*. So in order to buy back what Adam had lost in his relationship with God, Jesus had to become a man in a human body with a mind and emotions. He had to experience death on all levels: physically, mentally, and emotionally. And that's exactly what He did.

Hebrews 2:14–18 explains it this way.

> Since, therefore, [these His] children share in flesh and blood [in the physical nature of human beings], He [Himself] in a similar manner partook of the same [nature], that by [going through] death He might bring to nought and make of no effect him who had the power of death—that is, the devil— And also that He might deliver and completely set free all those who through the [haunting] fear of death were held in bondage throughout the whole course of their lives. For, as we all know, He [Christ] did not take hold of angels the fallen angels, to give them a helping and delivering hand], but He did take hold of the fallen] descendants of Abraham [to reach out to them a helping and delivering hand]. So it is evident that it was essential that He be made like His brethren in every respect, in order that He might become a merciful (sympathetic) and faithful High Priest in the things related to God, to make atonement and propitiation for the people's sins. For because He Himself [in His humanity] has suffered in being tempted (tested and tried), He is

able [immediately]to run to the cry of (assist, relieve) those who are being tempted and tested and tried [and who therefore are being exposed to suffering]. (AMPC)

Jesus was born a man in order to have the human experience necessary to reconcile us to God our Creator. He went through the process of death, on every level, physically, mentally, and emotionally. He conquered sin and death in the flesh to deliver and completely set us free.

Now remember, the relationship between God and man had to be based on a foundation of trust. And although man was given free will, it was paramount to choose God's word as truth. With that in mind, let's look to Jesus as our example of this intended relationship between a man and God.

In the gospel of John, Jesus is being challenged by the religious leaders of that day as He begins to explain His relationship with God the Father.

Jesus said to them, "If God were your Father, you would love me, for I came from God and I am here. I came not of my own accord, but he sent me. Why do you not understand what I say? It is because you cannot bear to hear my word. You are of your father the devil, and your will is to do your father's desires. He was a murderer from the beginning, and does not stand in the truth, because there is no truth in him. When he lies, he speaks out of his own character, for he is a liar and the father of lies. But because I tell the truth, you do not believe me. Which one of you convicts me of sin? If I tell the truth, why do you not believe me? Whoever is of

16

God hears the words of God. The reason why you do not hear them is that you are not of God." (John 8:42–47 ESV)

Not only did these religious leaders refuse to hear the words of truth spoken to them, but in the hardness of their hearts they even began to accuse Jesus Christ of having a demon.

The Jews answered him, "Are we not right in saying that you are a Samaritan and have a demon?" Jesus answered, "I do not have a demon, but I honor my Father, and you dishonor me. Yet I do not seek my own glory; there is One who seeks it, and he is the judge. Truly, truly, I say to you, if anyone keeps my word, he will never see death." The Jews said to him, "Now we know that you have a demon! Abraham died, as did the prophets, yet you say, 'If anyone keeps my word, he will never taste death.' Are you greater than our father Abraham, who died? And the prophets died! Who do you make yourself out to be?" Jesus answered, "If I glorify myself, my glory is nothing. It is my Father who glorifies me, of whom you say, 'He is our God.'" (John 8:48–54 ESV)

The Amplified Bible interprets verse 54 in this way;

Jesus answered, If I were to glorify Myself (magnify, praise, and honor Myself), I would have no real glory, for My glory would be nothing and worthless. [My honor must come to Me from My Father.] It is My Father Who glorifies Me [Who extols Me, magnifies, and praises Me], of Whom you say that He is your God. (John 8:54 AMP)

There is a great revelation in this verse and the reason for writing this book. I want to bring your attention to the fact that *Jesus said His honor must come to Him from His Father.* When Jesus was baptized by John the Baptist in the river Jordan, the Bible says the heavens were opened, the Spirit of God descended, and a voice was heard from heaven.

> And when Jesus was baptized, He went up at once out of the water; and behold, the heavens were opened, and he [John] saw the Spirit of God descending like a dove and alighting on Him. And behold, a voice from heaven said, This is My Son, My Beloved, in Whom I delight! (Matthew 3:16–17 AMP)

> It came to pass in those days that Jesus came from Nazareth of Galilee, and was baptized by John in the Jordan. And immediately, coming up from the water, He saw the heavens parting and the Spirit descending upon Him like a dove. Then a voice came from heaven, "You are My beloved Son, in whom I am well pleased." (Mark 1:9–11 NKJV)

> Now when all the people were baptized, Jesus was also baptized, and while He was praying, heaven was opened, and the Holy Spirit descended upon Him in bodily form like a dove, and a voice came out of heaven, "You are My beloved Son, in You I am well-pleased." (Luke 3:21–22 NASB)

Notice when Jesus was baptized, God did not say, "I give You honor and glory." Rather God said, "You are My beloved Son in whom I am well pleased." He spoke His love, approval, and acceptance to Jesus, which in turn honored and glorified Him! The Father's words imparted an identity to Jesus. That voice of power that we just read about in Genesis that created the entire universe was declared over His Son in such a way that Jesus was established in His identity with His Father! That's so powerful! It's a profound truth that every believer needs to have a revelation of. Remember, Jesus said His honor must come to Him from His Father. He knew that His true glory and honor came from the love, approval, and acceptance that only God His Father could give. This truth was all He needed to live and walk out His destiny. These powerful words from His Father are what established Jesus to be secure in His identity with His Father and in their relationship.

Not only did the words of God impart and establish an identity to His Son, but in addition, the words, "You are My Beloved Son in Whom I am well pleased," actually made a covering of honor and glory for Him!

The apostle Peter confirms this truth when speaking of the encounter he had with God the Father on the Mount of Transfiguration. The account is recorded in the gospels of Matthew and Luke, and it happened this way.

Peter, James, and John were led by Jesus up on a high mountain by themselves when, right before their eyes, Jesus was transformed in His appearance to such a degree that His face shone like the sun and His clothing glowed as light.

> And was transfigured before them: and his face did shine as the sun, and his raiment was white as the light. (Matthew 17:2 KJV)

> And as he was praying, the appearance of his face was transformed, and his clothes became dazzling white. (Luke 9:29 NLT)

As was characteristic of Peter's bold personality, he began to speak about how good it was to be there. But while he was speaking, a bright cloud overshadowed them, and they heard the voice of God. The sound was so awesome that they fell on their faces with fear.

> While he yet spake, behold, a bright cloud overshadowed them: and behold a voice out of the cloud, which said, This is my beloved Son, in whom I am well pleased; hear ye him. And when the disciples heard it, they fell on their face, and were sore afraid. (Matthew 17:5–6 KJV)

> But even as he was saying this, a cloud overshadowed them, and terror gripped them as the cloud covered them. Then a voice from the cloud said, "This is my Son, my Chosen One. Listen to him." (Luke 9:34–35 NLT)

This was the eyewitness account of Christ's brilliant transformation and glorification as seen and heard by the three disciples who were closest to Him. Then some forty years later when Peter is writing to encourage believers in their faith, we find him recounting this amazing event as recorded in 2 Peter.

> For when He was invested with honor and glory from God the Father and a voice was borne to Him by the [splendid] Majestic Glory [in the bright cloud that overshadowed Him, saying], This is My *beloved Son* in Whom I am well pleased and delight. (2 Peter 1:17 AMP)

> For He received from God the Father honor and glory when such a voice came to Him from the

Excellent Glory: "This is My beloved Son, in whom I am well pleased." (2 Peter 1:17 NKJV)

For he received from God [the] Father honour and glory, such a voice being uttered to him by the excellent glory: This is my beloved Son, in whom I have found my delight. (2 Peter 1:17 DARBY)

He received honor and glory from God the Father when the voice came to him from the Majestic Glory, saying, "This is my Son, whom I love; with him I am well pleased." (2 Peter 1:17 NIV)

Did you catch that? The key word here is *when*. *When* the voice of God the Father spoke, that's when honor and glory was released, imparted, and transferred to Jesus!

The Greek word here for "honor" is *timē,* which means to give a value to, to give a fixed price, or to give reverence. The definition also suggests that it is something precious. The Greek word for "glory" in this verse is *doxa*, which means to always have a good opinion concerning one, resulting in praise, honor, dignity, splendor, and majesty!

So God is telling us that *when* He spoke, "This is my Beloved Son, whom I love; with him I am well pleased," He was imparting honor and glory to Jesus that literally transmitted a covering of value, reverence, majesty, dignity, and splendor!

We find another confirmation to the truth that honor and glory were imparted to Jesus from God the Father in Hebrews chapter 5.

For every high priest taken from among men is appointed for men in things pertaining to God,

> that he may offer both gifts and sacrifices for sins. 2 He can have compassion on those who are ignorant and going astray, since he himself is also subject to weakness. 3 Because of this he is required as for the people, so also for himself, to offer sacrifices for sins. 4 And no man takes this honor to himself, but he who is called by God, just as Aaron was. 5 So also Christ did not glorify Himself to become High Priest, but it was He who said to Him: "You are My Son, Today I have begotten You." (Hebrews 5:1–5 NKJV)

This passage is talking about Jesus becoming our High Priest. I want to bring your attention in particular to verse 4. It says that the office of High Priest is not appointed by man, but rather it is an office that is called by God. Now notice the verse goes on to say, "no man takes this *honor* to himself." Then in verse 5 we read, "so also Christ did not *glorify* Himself to become High Priest." Notice the two words that are used interchangeably, honor and glory. In other words, it could say no man takes this glory to himself but he who is called by God. This is so important! The verse says Christ did not honor or glorify Himself, but it was He who said to Him: "You are My Son. Today I have begotten You."

This is a direct reference to the scriptures already mentioned when God spoke these words at the baptism of Jesus as recorded in Matthew 3:17, Mark 1:11, and Luke 3:22 in addition to the references in Matthew 17:5, Mark 9:7, and Luke 9:35 when Peter, James, and John witnessed the transfiguration of Jesus on the mountain. All these passages are an absolute confirmation of the truth that Jesus was honored and glorified *when* God spoke and affirmed that Jesus was His Son in whom He was well pleased! God's words honored Jesus. God's words glorified Jesus.

So Jesus, the man, was baptized with the Holy Spirit and given the Father's words of love and approval that imparted honor and glory to Him. This enabled Him to walk out the destiny He was called to. It was the power of the Spirit and the words from His Father that caused Him to withstand the temptations of the devil while in the wilderness. It was the words of approval, acceptance, and love that enabled Jesus to endure such blatant criticism from the religious leaders of His day. It was the Father's words transmitted to Jesus that empowered Him to endure from sinners such grievous opposition and bitter hostility, as the writer of Hebrews states. And it was these significantly powerful words spoken by God the Father that enabled Jesus to lay down His life, to be sharply rejected, mockingly ridiculed, vulgarly spat on, violently struck, brutally whipped, and mercilessly nailed to a cross for the sins of all mankind. That's our Savior and the power of the word of God!

The Father's words of unconditional love toward His Son are what gave Jesus the fortitude to choose God's will to die for mankind. The mental and emotional strength needed to choose God's will was established on the foundation that God His Father was well pleased with Him. The power in those words was enough because they imparted honor and glory to Jesus. Jesus knew His honor *must* come from His Father. He was clothed with glory and honor that comes from God alone. There is no other source in this universe that can impart glory, honor, and dignity into a person's life to such a degree that it causes an eternal transformation.

The glory and honor lost by Adam had been given to Jesus the man.

GLORY AND HONOR
GIVEN TO MAN

In the entire chapter of John 17, we are given a beautiful account of Jesus talking with the Father. It is absolutely my favorite passage of the entire Bible. His heart's dedication and love toward God and His undeniable passion for mankind are so wonderfully expressed and revealed to us. I believe this passage is one of the most meaningful narrations for believers because of its content and because it is one of the last things Christ spoke to His disciples before going to the cross. The entire chapter is amazing, but I want to draw your attention specifically to verse 22, where Jesus makes a profound statement. He says that we are given the same glory He received from the Father!

> I have given to them the glory and honor which You have given Me, that they may be one [even] as We are one: I in them and You in Me, in order that they may become one and perfectly united, that the world may know and [definitely] recognize that You sent Me and that You have loved them [even] as You have loved Me. (John 17:22–23 AMPC)

> The glory which You have given Me I have given to them, that they may be one, just as We are one; I in them and You in Me, that they may be perfected in unity, so that the world may know that You sent

Me, and loved them, even as You have loved Me.
(John 17:22–23 NASB)

And I have given to them the clearness, that thou
hast given to me, that they be one, as we be one; I in
them, and thou in me, that they be ended into one;
and that the world know, that thou sentest me, and
hast loved them, as thou hast loved also me. (John
17:22–23 WYC)

When Jesus said, "I have given to them the glory and honor that You
have given to Me," He was talking about the glory, honor, majesty,
and dignity that Jesus received from the Father! Did you hear that?
We have been given the same glory and honor because we have been
placed into Christ! The honor and glory that Adam lost was restored
back to man through Christ.

But God, who is rich in mercy, because of His great
love with which He loved us, even when we were
dead in trespasses, made us alive together with
Christ (by grace you have been saved), and raised
us up together, and made us sit together in the
heavenly places in Christ Jesus, that in the ages to
come He might show the exceeding riches of His
grace in His kindness toward us in Christ Jesus. For
by grace you have been saved through faith, and
that not of yourselves; it is the gift of God, not of
works, lest anyone should boast. (Ephesians 2:4-9
NKJV)

Oh, the heart of our Father is so beautifully revealed in this passage.
I love how it begins with, "But God." But God, so rich in His mercy
and in order to satisfy His great and wonderful and intense love, even
when we were dead in sin, made us alive together with Christ. He

gave us the very life of Christ! God gave us the same new life with which He quickened Christ when He raised Him from the dead! He raised us up from death. He raised us up together and made us sit together, giving us joint seating with Christ! We are seated together with Christ in the heavenly realm. The reason God did this is so in the ages to come, He would clearly demonstrate the immeasurable riches of favor in His goodness and kindness of heart toward us in Christ Jesus! There is absolutely no denying the heart of God toward man.

Now remember, Adam lost his identity in the garden. He lost sight of who he was and the relationship he shared with God. When we receive Jesus by faith and the sacrifice He made on the cross for our sin, we are placed into Christ. Because of God's great love, He made us alive together with Christ. Now our position *in* Christ is our new identity. We have been given a new nature. The Bible says our sin nature that was inherited through Adam has now been crucified with Christ. We are no longer identified with our old sin nature, but instead we have a new nature in Christ. We've been recreated in Christ Jesus. It is the great exchange. Jesus, who knew no sin, became sin that we might become the righteousness of God in Christ. That is why God placed us into Christ.

> Therefore, if anyone is in Christ, he is a new creation. The old has passed away; behold, the new has come. All this is from God, who through Christ reconciled us to himself and gave us the ministry of reconciliation; that is, in Christ God was reconciling the world to himself, not counting their trespasses against them, and entrusting to us the message of reconciliation. Therefore, we are ambassadors for Christ, God making his appeal through us. We implore you on behalf of Christ, be reconciled to God. For our sake he made him to be sin who

knew no sin, so that in him we might become the righteousness of God. (2 Corinthians 5:17–21 ESV)

Putting us into Christ was God's way of reconciling the relationship with man that He lost with Adam. He put us into perfection. He gave us righteousness, the right standing that Christ has. Oh the wonderful grace and love of our God!

> I in them, and You in Me; that they may be made perfect in one, and that the world may know that You have sent Me, and have loved them as You have loved Me. (John 17:22 NKJV)

In this verse the Lord goes on to say that as believers have the revelation of the glory and honor given to us, we will become united. We must see ourselves in this truth and in this light. Furthermore, we must also see each other in this way. We must see ourselves and others as valuable and honorable people. We must see our real identity, who we really are in Christ. Can you imagine if everyone esteemed each other in this way? Jesus prayed that all believers would come to this truth.

Interestingly, the Wycliffe version uses the word *clearness* for the word *glory*.

> And I have given to them the clearness, that thou hast given to me, that they be one, as we be one. (John 17:22 WYC)

> The glory which You have given Me I have given to them, that they may be one, just as We are one. (John 17:22 NASB)

If we consider the covering Adam and Eve had in the garden before eating of the fruit, this gives us a more accurate understanding. Their perspective was clear. They were seeing clearly. In this verse, when Jesus says, "I have given to them the honor and glory," He is saying, "I have given them clearness. I have given them the ability to see clearly again." The honor and glory cause us to see clearly. The honor and glory give us the right perspective! When we understand our relationship with God through the finished redemptive work of Christ, we see clearly. The right relationship brings clarity. We actually step into a right relationship with God from the moment we receive Christ. The Bible says we become a new creation, old things pass away, and all things become new. Our spirit comes alive. It is quickened. It is made alive, and we begin to see the truth. The more we come into a personal relationship and understanding of who God is and how He really sees us, we begin to see clearly. It is the truth that sets us free. There is only one truth, and it is Christ. He is the Way, the Truth, and the Life. The word *the* is used specifically because it denotes the following noun as definite and unique. There is no other way, there is no other truth, and there is no other life.

It is important to clarify that the Bible talks about glory in many ways. First, as we just read, Jesus said He gave us the same glory that God the Father had given Him. Glory in this sense is from the Greek word *doxa,* which, as mentioned before, means to always have a good opinion concerning one, resulting in praise, honor, dignity, splendor, and majesty. And we know that Jesus received this glory (doxa) from the Father when He said, "This is My Beloved Son in whom I am well pleased." God spoke these words first at the baptism of Jesus as recorded in the gospels of Matthew, Mark, and Luke.

> And suddenly a voice came from heaven, saying, "This is My beloved Son, in whom I am well pleased." (Matthew 3:17 NKJV)

Then a second time on the mountaintop known as the mount of transfiguration, God the Father declares:

> And a cloud came and overshadowed them; and a voice came out of the cloud, saying, "This is My beloved Son. Hear Him!" (Mark 9:7 NKJV)

On both occasions, God's words declared that He always has a good opinion of His Son, resulting in honor, dignity, and glory. The significance of these words is profound. We know that God spoke innumerable times to prophets and kings throughout the Old Testament, but the only time He spoke in the New Testament, the new covenant between God and man was to honor and glorify His Son. Think about that. What an impact these words had. Their value is immeasurable considering they are the only words God spoke audibly after Christ's birth.

The third time God spoke in an audible voice was recorded in John chapter 12. It was the day Jesus entered Jerusalem for the Passover Feast and the people laid out palm branches as He rode in on a donkey. In verse 23 He told His disciples His hour had come to fulfill God's purpose. He said it in this way:

> But Jesus answered them, saying, "The hour has come that the Son of Man should be glorified. Most assuredly, I say to you, unless a grain of wheat falls into the ground and dies, it remains alone; but if it dies, it produces much grain. He who loves his life will lose it, and he who hates his life in this world will keep it for eternal life. If anyone serves Me, let him follow Me; and where I am, there My servant will be also. If anyone serves Me, him My Father will honor. "Now My soul is troubled, and what shall I say? 'Father, save Me from this hour'? But

for this purpose I came to this hour. Father, glorify Your name." Then a voice came from heaven, saying, "I have both glorified it and will glorify it again." (John 12:23–28 NKJV)

Jesus began by saying that He was about to be glorified. Now we know that He was glorified when God spoke at His baptism and when He was transfigured on the mountain, so Jesus was already honored and dignified by the words of His Father, but now Jesus is saying that His glory would be made manifest by His death, burial, and resurrection. It would be made known. He explains that in order to be glorified, he will have to die. He will lay down His life and allow Himself to be crucified. Then we see the beautiful picture of the love and devotion between the Father and the Son as Jesus reveals the struggle of His decision in knowing what He was about to face. We understand that He had to come to earth as a man with feelings and weaknesses to take back what Adam had forfeited. Jesus said His soul was troubled. His mind and will and emotions were troubled at the great suffering He would have to endure to redeem the penalty of mankind's sin. He knew He would actually have to take our sin upon Himself. But the beautiful thing about Jesus is that His love and devotion to His Father outweighed the agony of the horrific sin and death He would experience. He says, "Father glorify *Your* name." He didn't say, "Glorify Me." His heart was completely devoted to do God's will. He worshiped and served His Father. He was completely selfless, even unto death. Oh, what a Savior!

Jesus said if we serve Him, we are to follow Him. In other words, be selfless as well. The word *serve* in this verse is the Greek word *diakoneō,* and it means to attend to anything that may serve another's interests. Jesus "served" the Father by choosing to do what was in God's interest. Jesus chose God's will over His own. It was God's will for Jesus to die for mankind. He honored God, and God honored Him. It's a beautiful picture of true love.

In John 17:23 Jesus explains that He has given us the glory and honor that God has given Him so that believers would be one just as Jesus and the Father are one. To be one is to be in union and concord, to be in a state of agreement, in covenant. To be one is to be in perfect harmony with each other.

> The glory which You have given Me I have given to them, that they may be one, just as We are one; I in them and You in Me, that they may be perfected in unity, so that the world may know that You sent Me, and loved them, even as You have loved Me. (John 17:22–23 NASB)

Unity among believers is paramount for the world to recognize the truth that God sent Jesus to redeem mankind. We understand that unity among believers is a necessity. As it is now, the world sees division among believers. This tells us that the knowledge of the glory Jesus has given is absolutely necessary and vital to be received and understood by all believers. We must know we have been given the same glory that Jesus was given. It's overwhelming to realize this truth, but it is in fact the truth. Jesus explains that as we receive His glory and honor, there are three things that will occur. First, believers will become one, meaning we will be perfectly united. Second, this unity among believers will cause the world to know that God did in fact send Jesus, and finally, the world will know that God loves them even as He loves His Son Jesus. We must receive the glory Jesus has given us!

So how do we receive the glory Christ offers? Well, we know that we receive the word of God by faith. So by faith we believe and receive the glory Jesus says he has given us. Then Jesus goes on and makes an incredible request of the Father.

In verse 24 Jesus asks the Father an amazing question.

> Father, I desire that they also whom you have given Me may be with Me where I am, that they may behold My glory which You have given Me; for You loved Me before the foundation of the world. (John 17:24 NKJV)

Jesus asks that believers be with Him where He is in order to see the glory that God had given Him! Now Jesus already told us that He has given us the same glory that God had given Him. Then He says He wants us to see that glory. He wants us to see this beautiful, intimate love and honor and glory that He and the Father share!

Some may say, "Well sure, we'll see the glory of God when we go to heaven," and that is true. But we have to ask ourselves, "What is Jesus actually saying here?" Why would He tell the Father He desires that we be with Him where He is so that we can see His glory? Scripture tells us that we will be with Jesus in heaven and see God in all His glory, but in this verse, Jesus is not just talking about seeing His glory in heaven. He is saying that He desires for us to see His glory now!

The Bible tells us in Ephesians 2:6 that we are seated with Christ in heavenly places. In the spirit, we are already with Christ. Colossians 1:3 says our new real life is hidden with Christ in God. And where is Christ? John 1:18 tells us that Jesus is in the bosom of the Father. The bosom is the place closest to one's heart. It's the place of greatest intimacy with our Father. We've been placed into Christ, into the place of the most holy and blessed intimacy with God, because we are in Christ. We are in the bosom of God.

So as believers, we're already with Jesus where He prayed we would be, so we would see His glory. The word *see* in this verse is the Greek word *theoreo,* which means to look at, to behold, to perceive with the eyes, to find out by seeing. It's wonderful to be able to see and discover the glory Jesus has. As we behold His glory, we discover how beautiful, majestic, good, loving, and holy He is. But the wonderful thing about it and the reason Jesus wants us to see *His* glory now is because He just told us that He has given us the *same* glory! So when we see His glory, we are ultimately seeing what has been given to us! We discover the treasure of Christ within us and upon us. God wants us to see that we have been given honor, majesty, and dignity.

> For all of you who were baptized into Christ have clothed yourselves with Christ. (Galatians 3:27 NIV)

We have been given the same glory and honor that the Father gave to Jesus. When we see Jesus in all His glory, we will see what is within us! We will see ourselves clothed in majesty and dignity. Now that's a truth to receive!

RIGHTEOUSNESS REVEALED

The book of Romans is the first epistle written in the New Testament because it clearly explains the foundation of Christianity, which is salvation by grace through faith in Christ. Man is reconciled to God and put into right standing with Him only through faith in what Christ has accomplished for us. When Adam sinned in the garden by choosing to disobey God, death spread to all mankind. Everyone born after Adam inherited a sin nature, hence all mankind. We are not sinners because we sin. We are sinners because we have a sin nature.

> When Adam sinned, sin entered the world. Adam's sin brought death, so death spread to everyone, for everyone sinned. (Romans 5:17 NLT)

Many people don't understand why they need saving. In their hearts, they believe they are good people, so they don't see the need for a Savior. But the problem is the sin nature that was inherited by every person born since Adam. No matter how good a person is, there is still a sin nature within him or her. The only way for that to change is through the sinless blood of Christ, the Son of God. There is no other way. Jesus is the way, the truth, and the life.

Remember, God told Adam that if he ate the fruit (chose his own way of doing things), he would die. Even though Adam was given the free will to make his own choices, he had to trust that what God told him was the truth. It had to be a relationship based on trust, knowing that God had his best interest at heart. When Adam chose to eat the fruit, he did indeed die, but not in the sense that he suddenly dropped dead. Rather, it was the process of death that was initiated by Adam's decision to sin. The word *sin* is the Greek word *hamartia,* which means to miss the mark or to err. Again, man's relationship to God has to be established on the fact that God has man's best interest in mind. If He says not to do something, we must trust that it is for our good. The death that God spoke of was the result of sin and all the miseries it encompasses, physically, mentally, and emotionally. After the fall, God drove Adam and Eve out of the garden, not to separate Himself from them but because of His great mercy. You might ask how that is merciful. Well remember, there were two trees in the midst of the garden, the tree of the knowledge of good and evil, and the tree of life. If Adam had eaten from the tree of life after the fall, he and everyone born after him would have lived forever with the sin nature and all the horrible effects it brings. That's the mercy of our God because He had a better plan in mind. He purposed for us to be reconciled back into an intimate relationship with Him through the perfection of His Son.

Christ came to redeem mankind. He was sent by God to purchase back all that Adam had forfeited through the deception of Satan. The Bible says that God disarmed the powers that were against us and made a public display of them by triumphing over them in Him, in the cross. When Jesus hung on that cross, He took all the sin of humanity that separated the Creator from His creation and reconciled us back to our Father. Because of His great love, He gave His life, His own blood, His sinless blood. And by His selfless sacrifice, He secured a complete redemption and an everlasting release for us. It was an eternal deliverance for all who would choose to accept Jesus as their Savior. And when you choose to receive Him as your Savior, you are given His righteousness.

What does it mean to have righteousness? Righteousness is a gift that says you are in right relationship with God. It has to do with our position of being in Christ. We are declared righteous, in right standing, acceptable and approved of by God because of our placement in Christ. The Greek word for righteousness is *dikaiosune,* which literally means right action. Because we believe and have faith in Jesus Christ and His finished work on the cross to redeem us, we are put into a right relationship with God. All the requirements necessary to be in a right relationship with God were met in Christ. Because of our sin nature, we could never meet the requirements. Only the spotless Son of God could and did. Righteousness has nothing to do with doing right. It is a gift from God. We are no more righteous after being a Christian and walking with God for fifty years than we are one minute after we are born again. We are not righteous because of any works we do or because of any obedience to the law. This mind-set of upholding the law was evident in the scribes and Pharisees of Jesus's day and is unfortunately preached in many churches today. The Bible says man's righteousness is as filthy rags. It is prideful to think we could do something to merit a right relationship with God. We could never do what Christ did, which was to live a sinless life. We could never rid ourselves of our sin nature. That is why God sent Jesus in the first place—to save us from our sins. We could never earn our right standing with God. It is all about Jesus, and it is only about Jesus. We must keep our minds set on who Christ is for us. He and He alone is our righteousness. We must be careful that because we are in ministry or go on a missions trip or pray and fast and read our Bibles or volunteer at church or give generously, or whatever other work we do "for God" does not become something that we take pride in. Again, it is always and only about Jesus. He came and did what we never could do for ourselves. We thank God for His amazing grace that we can now live acceptable, approved, and in right standing with Him because we have received Christ as our Savior. Righteousness is an awesome and wonderful gift that we are privileged to receive, simply because of our belief in Christ. Jesus said for us to receive the kingdom, you must become as a little child. I love how this is explained in Isaiah 55:1 of the Amplified Bible:

> Wait and listen, everyone who is thirsty! Come to the waters; and he who has no money, come, buy and eat! Yes, come, buy [priceless, spiritual] wine and milk without money and without price [simply for the self-surrender that accepts the blessing].

Man's pride has a hard time receiving the simplicity of the gospel. Pride says I must do something and I will do something to prove myself. It takes a humble person, a humble heart, to receive the free gift of righteousness through Christ. It is an overwhelming revelation when we come to the understanding that Christ took all our sin upon Himself so we could come into relationship with God. He set us free to enter a relationship with our Father, our Creator, and God Almighty. We can come freely before God without fear, guilt, or even the sense of sin. It only takes faith in what Christ has done for us. It is a childlike faith. It is a heart of humility. We come to Christ and receive all He has done for us simply for the self-surrender that accepts the blessing!

The apostle Paul expressed the truth of righteousness this way.

> For no person will be justified (made righteous, acquitted, and judged acceptable) in His sight by observing the works prescribed by the Law. For [the real function of] the Law is to make men recognize and be conscious of sin [a]not mere perception, but an acquaintance with sin which works toward repentance, faith, and holy character]. But now the righteousness of God has been revealed independently and altogether apart from the Law,

although actually it is attested by the Law and
the Prophets, Namely, the righteousness of God
which comes by believing with personal trust and
confident reliance on Jesus Christ. [And it is meant]
for all who believe. For there is no distinction, Since
all have sinned and are falling short of the honor
and glory which God bestows and receives. All are
justified and made upright and in right standing
with God, freely and gratuitously by His grace
(His unmerited favor and mercy), through the
redemption which is [provided] in Christ Jesus.
(Romans 3:20–24 AMP)

Therefore, just as sin entered the world through one
man, and death through sin, and in this way death
came to all people, because all sinned. (Romans
5:12 NIV)

For if because of one man's trespass (lapse, offense)
death reigned through that one, much more surely
will those who receive [God's] overflowing grace
(unmerited favor) and the free gift of righteousness
[putting them into right standing with Himself]
reign as kings in life through the one Man Jesus
Christ (the Messiah, the Anointed One). (Romans
5:17 AMP)

For the sin of this one man, Adam, caused death to
rule over many. But even greater is God's wonderful
grace and his gift of righteousness, for all who receive
it will live in triumph over sin and death through
this one man, Jesus Christ. (Romans 5:1 NLT)

Notice this verse says that the sin of Adam caused death to rule over many. Death is the result of sin. One translation says death held sway over, meaning it had a controlling influence over man, which we could not escape. This includes death in our bodies, our minds, and our emotions, death in every aspect. Again, this all took place after the fall of man and was never God's intention or His plan for mankind. But praise God, the verse goes on to say that as we receive God's wonderful grace and gift of righteousness, we will live in victory over sin and death through Christ.

> And the result of God's gracious gift is very different from the result of that one man's sin. For Adam's sin led to condemnation, but God's free gift leads to our being made right with God, even though we are guilty of many sins. For the sin of this one man, Adam, caused death to rule over many. But even greater is God's wonderful grace and his gift of righteousness, for all who receive it will live in triumph over sin and death through this one man, Jesus Christ. Yes, Adam's one sin brings condemnation for everyone, but Christ's one act of righteousness brings a right relationship with God and new life for everyone. (Romans 5:16–18 NLT)

Sometimes even the way we look at faith can become a work. When believers are faced with a difficulty, you might hear things like, "Just have faith," or "You don't have enough faith," or "You need more faith." This causes people to begin to look at themselves, which in turn brings about an incorrect focus. The focus is toward themselves and what they have or have not done, haven't done enough, have done too much, or have not done the right way! That's exhausting! The focus begins to be back on man when it has nothing to do with man. The work has been done. It's all about Christ and His finished work. He did it all. It was a complete work so our focus is only and must only be on Christ. Christ did not die in vain. Hanging there on that cross, knowing the work had been accomplished, Jesus cried out in a loud voice, "It is finished!" And He meant it.

Man continues to try to add to redemption because we haven't understood what the completed work entails and what it truly means. Man seems to feel the need to have to add to the finished work and consequently slips back into having to do, having to accomplish, having to measure up to a certain standard, when Christ is the standard. Christ met the standard. Christ fulfilled the standard. That is why Jesus came—to set man free, to undo what the fall of Adam caused. Now man is justified or brought into a right relationship with God, not by his own efforts to be right but only by faith in what Jesus accomplished. This is the good news and the wonderful grace God offers every person regardless of who he or she is or what he or she has done or has not done.

There is a popular verse in the book of Habakkuk where the prophet tells the people to write the vision and make it plain for it is set for an appointed time. And though it tarry, wait for it will come to pass on its appointed day. The verse that follows reads:

> Look at the proud; his soul is not straight or right within him, but the [rigidly] just and the [uncompromisingly] righteous man shall [a]live by his faith and in his faithfulness. (Habakkuk 2:4 AMPC)

> "Look at the proud! They trust in themselves, and their lives are crooked. But the righteous will live by their faithfulness to God." (Habakkuk 2:4 NLT)

(Lo! the soul of him, who is unbelieving, shall not be right within himself; but the just, or the righteous, shall live by faith.) (Habakkuk 2:4 WYC)

This is an interesting verse because it points out that it is simply the pride of man that trusts in himself. It takes faith to trust in God when everything around you says it's a failure, there's no hope, or it's impossible. This word *soul* in the Wycliffe version is the Greek word *nephesh,* and it includes our mind and our will. When we depend on our strength, our ability, our timing, or our way of walking through this life, we are ultimately in unbelief. It is a crooked way of living. But the righteous live by faith. I love the way the Amplified Bible explains faith. It is defined as the "leaning of the entire personality on God in absolute trust and confidence in His power, wisdom, and goodness." When our perspective is correct as to how God really feels about us, we will walk by faith, trusting in our Creator, knowing He always has our best interest at heart.

> Therefore, since we have been made right in God's sight by faith, we have peace[a] with God because of what Jesus Christ our Lord has done for us. (Romans 5:1 NLT)

> Having been declared righteous, then, by faith, we have peace toward God through our Lord Jesus Christ. (Romans 5:1 YLT)

For us to be settled in the belief that we are righteous before God, we must rest. Staying in rest, staying in peace on the inside is the blessing of knowing we are the righteousness of God in Christ.

A NEW CREATION

As believers, we have become a new creation in Christ Jesus. We now have a recreated spirit. The old has passed away, and all things have been made new. We no longer have the sin nature, because now we have a new nature. It is the nature of God. We do not identify with our old nature, but we identify with our new nature, which has been created in true righteousness and holiness. I love that. It's not man's righteousness and holiness but Christ's righteousness and holiness. That is our new nature and our new identity.

> And put on the new nature (the regenerate self) created in God's image, [Godlike] in true righteousness and holiness. (Ephesians 4:24 AMPC)

Our spirit has been made alive as a new created being, and we have become one spirit with Christ. When we receive Jesus, the Holy Spirit comes to abide with our spirit. We have become a dwelling place of God. We are the temple of the Holy Spirit, so we are a home for God to live in. You could say He's at home in us. The intimacy that was once lost has been restored, and we have become God's personal dwelling place. The Lord calls it a "fixed abode," meaning that His dwelling place in us is established, anchored, and secure.

But he who is joined to the Lord becomes one spirit
with him. (1 Corinthians 6:17 ESV)

Jesus answered him, "If anyone loves me, he will
keep my word, and my Father will love him, and
we will come to him and make our home with him.
(John 14:23 ESV)

God is so passionate about wanting His children to know Him and
that His heart of love overflows toward us. The Holy Spirit lives
in every believer. It's a spirit-to-Spirit, heart-to-heart relationship
between man and Creator. The presence of God within is glorious
because He is glorious. There is nothing more wonderful, more
beautiful, more powerful, more holy, or more intimate. There are
just not enough or even adequate words to describe the splendor and
majesty of our God.

His presence within is an inner witness that assures us of His love
and affirms His acceptance and approval. The Holy Spirit within us
bears witness with our spirit that we are sons and daughters of God,
and our spirit now follows the leading of the Holy Spirit within.

For as many as are led by the Spirit of God, these
are sons of God. For you did not receive the spirit
of bondage again to fear, but you received the Spirit
of adoption by whom we cry out, "Abba, Father."
The Spirit Himself bears witness with our spirit that
we are children of God. (Romans 8:14–16 NKJV)

GLORY WITHIN

Several times in the New Testament, the apostle Paul refers to the mystery of the gospel. We find one of the references in Colossians 1.

> Of which I became a minister according to the stewardship from God which was given to me for you, to fulfill the word of God, the mystery which has been hidden from ages and from generations, but now has been revealed to His saints. To them God willed to make known what are the riches of the glory of this mystery among the Gentiles: which is Christ in you, the hope of glory. (Colossians 1:25–27 NKJV)

The Amplified Bible says it this way;

> To whom God was pleased to make known how great for the Gentiles are the riches of the glory of this mystery, which is Christ within and among you, the Hope of [realizing the] glory.

The New Living Translation says:

> For God wanted them to know that the riches and glory of Christ are for you Gentiles, too. And this

is the secret: Christ lives in you. This gives you
assurance of sharing his glory.

In Paul's letter to the Galatians, he begins by defending the gospel
of Christ and adamantly proclaims there is no other gospel. He even
goes so far as to say that anyone preaching anything other than what
Paul preached is accursed. He continues his letter by reminding us
that at one time, he exceeded most of his generation in the study
and observance of Jewish law and the traditions of his ancestors, so
much so that his passion drove him to persecute the church with a
determination to destroy it. You see, Paul had been part of a religious
system that believed in obeying every rule and Jewish regulation
perfectly for the purpose of being acceptable to God. And until
God knocked him off his horse, literally, and revealed the truth of
Christ, Paul prided himself on his spotless character, as he admits
in his letter to the Philippians.

> Though I also might have confidence in the flesh.
> If anyone else thinks he may have confidence in
> the flesh, I more so: circumcised the eighth day,
> of the stock of Israel, of the tribe of Benjamin, a
> Hebrew of the Hebrews; concerning the law, a
> Pharisee; concerning zeal, persecuting the church;
> concerning the righteousness which is in the law,
> blameless. (Philippians 3:4–6 NKJV)

Nevertheless, even in all his zeal, he tells us that God Almighty had
other plans.

Paul goes on to say that he was not taught the gospel of Christ by
man, but rather he received it by the revelation of Jesus Christ.
Did you hear that? It was through the revealing of Jesus Christ.
Even before Paul was born, God had chosen and called him by His
grace to proclaim the gospel to the gentiles. And the scripture says

this happened when God saw fit and was pleased to reveal His Son *within* Paul.

> But when it pleased him, that separated me [that parted me] from my mother's womb, and called by his grace, to show his Son in me, that I should preach him among the heathen, at once I drew me not to flesh and blood [anon I accorded not to flesh and blood]. (Galatians 1:15-16 WYC)

> But when it pleased God, who separated me from my mother's womb and called me through His grace, to reveal His Son in me, that I might preach Him among the Gentiles, I did not immediately confer with flesh and blood. (Galatians 1:15-16 NKJV)

The word *reveal* in this passage means to uncover, to lay open what has been veiled or covered up, to disclose, to make bare, to make known, to make manifest, to disclose what before was unknown.

Oh the wonders of God! He wants to reveal Himself. He wants us to know Him. He wants to make known that which was unknown. He wants us to know and understand Christ within us! Here we have a man, highly learned and zealous in the knowledge of Hebrew Scriptures, passionate in his determination to follow the law, relentless in his pursuit to persecute the followers of Jesus when suddenly Christ Himself stopped him in his tracks, asking, "Why do you persecute Me?"

This man, who adamantly believed he knew the truth, was confronted with the Truth! And with Paul's acknowledgment of Jesus as Lord, the Holy Spirit began to give him the revelation of Christ within him. The revelation Paul received was God's supernatural unveiling of Christ within. In verse 12, Paul said he did not receive the gospel from man, nor was it taught to him, but that it came by the revelation of Jesus Christ. Over the next thirty years, Paul wrote the majority of the New Testament proclaiming the gospel of Jesus Christ.

First Corinthians chapter 2 tells us that God's plan was once hidden, for if it had been known, the rulers of this present age would never have crucified the Lord Jesus, the Lord of glory. This amazing plan of God's had to be hidden from the powers of darkness or they would not have played right into God's plan to have Jesus crucified. It was only through the death and resurrection of Jesus that man has been given access to the Father. Man's redemption could only be secured through the perfection of His Son. But in the wisdom of God, no eye has seen, no hear has heard, neither has it entered into the heart of man all the things God has prepared for those who love Him. Yet these things are revealed by the Spirit.

> However, we speak wisdom among those who are mature, yet not the wisdom of this age, nor of the rulers of this age, who are coming to nothing. But we speak the wisdom of God in a mystery, the hidden wisdom which God ordained before the ages for our glory, which none of the rulers of this age knew; for had they known, they would not have crucified the Lord of glory. But as it is written: "Eye has not seen, nor ear heard, the things which God has prepared for those who love Him." But God has revealed them to us through His Spirit. For the Spirit searches all things, yes, the deep things of God. For what man knows the things of a man except the spirit of the man which is in him? Even so no one knows the things of God except the Spirit of God. Now we have received, not the spirit of the world, but the Spirit who is from God, that we

might know the things that have been freely given to us by God. These things we also speak, not in words which man's wisdom teaches but which the Holy Spirit teaches, comparing spiritual things with spiritual. (1 Corinthians 2:6-13 NKJV)

The Holy Spirit within will reveal the things that we have been freely given. So, just as Paul had a revelation of Christ within, the hope of glory, God wants us to see and know the glory that is within us! It is the same glory that was given to Christ Himself that has now been given to us.

Paul encourages believers with this truth as he writes his second letter to the church of Thessalonica.

> But we are bound to give thanks to God always for you, brethren beloved by the Lord, because God from the beginning chose you for salvation through sanctification by the Spirit and belief in the truth, to which He called you by our gospel, for the obtaining of the glory of our Lord Jesus Christ. (2 Thessalonians 2:13–14 NKJV)

> And we—we ought to give thanks to God always for you, brethren, beloved by the Lord, that God did choose you from the beginning to salvation, in sanctification of the Spirit, and belief of the truth, to which He did call you through our good news, to the acquiring of the glory of our Lord Jesus Christ. (2 Thessalonians 2:13–14 YLT)

> But we ought always to thank God for you, brothers and sisters loved by the Lord, because God chose you as firstfruits to be saved through the sanctifying

work of the Spirit and through belief in the truth.
He called you to this through our gospel that you
might share in the glory of our Lord Jesus Christ.
(2 Thessalonians 2:13–14 NIV)

Did you catch that? This verse tells us specifically that God called us through the gospel to obtain, acquire, and share in the glory of our Lord Jesus Christ! The mystery is Christ within, the hope of glory. It's the hope of realizing the glory within.

GLORY TO ANOTHER

For years I've heard people say that God will not share His glory with anyone. However, when I read that Jesus gave us the same glory that God gave Him, it would seem to be a contradiction. Well, we know God does not contradict Himself. He means exactly what He says. Let's look at the scripture that people refer to about God sharing His glory. It's found in Isaiah 42:8.

> I am the Lord, that is My name; And My glory I will not give to another, Nor My praise to carved images. (Isaiah 42:8 NKJV)

God says He will not give His glory to another. However, if we study this word *another*, we find it is the Hebrew word *acher,* which means, other, following, different, and strange. Over and over again the Bible refers to other gods or another god. When this phrase is used, the context of what is being said is referring to graven and carved images or idols. God's first commandment to the Israelites was that they would have no other gods before them. Again "other gods" is referring to anything that would come before God. Or we could say anything that would come before Him in their lives. I like the way the apostle John says it in 1 John 5:

> Little children, keep yourselves from idols (false gods)—[from anything and everything that would

occupy the place in your heart due to God, from any
sort of substitute for Him that would take first place
in your life]. Amen (so let it be). (1 John 5:21 AMP)

So in Isaiah 42 when God says He will not give His glory to another,
He is referring to other gods as well. Now the exciting news is that
as believers, we are not "other gods," but we are sons and daughters
of God. God will not give His glory to another, but through Christ,
God will give and has given His glory and honor to His sons and
daughters! We have been placed into Christ, and the Holy Spirit
dwells in us, lives in us, and directs our lives. Because we have the
spirit of God within us, we are called the sons of God. Romans 8:14
says, "For those who are led by the Spirit of God are sons of God."
In John 1 we are told that for those who did receive and welcome
Christ, He gave them the privilege to become the children of God.
We are sons and daughters of the Most High God!

In Isaiah 42:8, the word *glory* is the Hebrew word *kabowd*. Its
meaning is glory, honor, abundance, riches, splendor, dignity, and
reputation.

As mentioned before, in John 17:22 the word for glory is the Greek
word *doxa*. Its meaning is always a good opinion concerning one,
resulting in praise, honor, and glory, dignity, majesty, a most glorious
condition, and a most exalted state.

When God said He will not give His glory to another, He was not
talking about believers. We are not "another."

> I have given to them the glory and honor which You
> have given Me, that they may be one [even] as We
> are one. (John 17:22 AMP)

These are the words of Christ Himself.

Now I need to make a clarification here in regard to the word *glory* and its meaning. When speaking of the glory that Christ has given us, He is talking about honor and dignity, which gives value to a person. This glory places significance on an individual. This is paramount to our understanding of what has been given to us through Christ. Glory in this sense means to always have a good opinion concerning someone. Because we have been placed into Christ, God always has a good opinion of us that imparts honor and dignity and value to our person. The glory and honor we are given places us in a position of importance, worth, and significance. It is our position in Christ. That's a truth that needs to be realized and established in every believer's heart.

Now when we speak of the word *glory* in the sense of praise, it is God and God only who gets all the "glory," meaning all the credit and all the praise. We are nothing without God. We take no credit for being in Christ. We cannot even take credit for getting saved. It is God who draws us to His Son. We abide and remain in the truth that God alone is Creator and we are His creation. He alone gets all the credit. He alone gets all the glory.

Now we know that initially Adam and Eve had a covering from their Creator that established their identity and gave them security and peace within themselves, with each other, and in their relationship to their Creator. They were made in the image of God and clothed with the glory of God. Their identity was clear.

In the same way, as born-again believers in Christ Jesus, our glory is in knowing we have the love and approval and acceptance of our Father! Just as Jesus received honor and glory from God the Father, in the same way, we are to receive the same honor and glory from the Father because we have been placed into Jesus Christ. *We've been placed into the Beloved!*

Even as he chose us in him before the foundation of the world, that we should be holy and blameless before him. In love he predestined us[a] for adoption as sons through Jesus Christ, according to the purpose of his will, to the praise of his glorious grace, with which he has blessed us in the Beloved. (Ephesians 1:4–6 ESV)

Even as [in His love] He chose us [actually picked us out for Himself as His own] in Christ before the foundation of the world, that we should be holy (consecrated and set apart for Him) and blameless in His sight, even above reproach, before Him in love. For He foreordained us (destined us, planned in love for us) to be adopted (revealed) as His own children through Jesus Christ, in accordance with the purpose of His will [[a]because it pleased Him and was His kind intent]— [So that we might be] to the praise and the commendation of His glorious grace (favor and mercy), which He so freely bestowed on us in the Beloved. (Ephesians 1:4–6 AMPC)

I love how the Amplified Version says that it was God's kind intent to adopt us as His children through Christ. Oh, the kindness of God is matchless!

We've been crowned with glory and honor. We've been given the same honor and glory that Jesus was given. It is the highest order of honor that can be given to a person.

Remember Jesus said, "My honor must come to Me from My Father," and God said, "You are My beloved Son in whom I am well pleased." He spoke His love and approval and acceptance to Jesus, which honored and glorified Him. He was clothed with the glory of the Father. Now in the same way, we are clothed with glory and honor in knowing we have the love and approval and acceptance of our Father. God is well pleased with us!

RECEIVING THE WORD

> May grace (God's favor) and peace (which is perfect well-being, all necessary good, all spiritual prosperity, and freedom from fears and agitating passions and moral conflicts) be multiplied to you in [the full, personal, precise, and correct] knowledge of God and of Jesus our Lord. (2 Peter 1:2 AMPC)

I like how this verse says the precise and correct knowledge. As we come to know the truth about whom God really is and Jesus our Lord, God's favor and peace will increase in our lives.

In John chapter 8 we find Jesus talking with a crowd people about truth. In verse 12 He makes this statement:

> Jesus spoke to the people once more and said, "I am the light of the world. If you follow me, you won't have to walk in darkness, because you will have the light that leads to life." (John 8:12 NLT)

Light shows you the way. Light brings clarity. It shows you the truth. Jesus declares He is that light that shows the way to truth. Then for the next forty-six verses, the religious leaders began to challenge who Jesus was and what He said. It seems ironic that the people who should have recognized and believed that Jesus was the Son of God were the very ones who doubted and questioned Him.

> Then they said to Him, "Where is Your Father?" Jesus answered, "You know neither Me nor My Father. If you had known Me, you would have known My Father also." These words Jesus spoke in the treasury, as He taught in the temple; and no one laid hands on Him, for His hour had not yet come. 21 Then Jesus said to them again, "I am going away, and you will seek Me, and will die in your sin. Where I go you cannot come." (John 8:19–21 NKJV)

When Jesus says that they will die in their sin, He is telling the Pharisees that they will ultimately die in their sin of unbelief because they do not believe that He is who He says He is.

> And He said to them, "You are from beneath; I am from above. You are of this world; I am not of this world. Therefore I said to you that you will die in your sins; for if you do not believe that I am He, you will die in your sins." Then they said to Him, "Who are You?" And Jesus said to them, "Just what I have been saying to you from the beginning. I have many things to say and to judge concerning you, but He who sent Me is true; and I speak to the world those things which I heard from Him." They did not understand that He spoke to them of the Father. Then Jesus said to them, "When you lift up the Son of Man, then you will know that I am He, and that I do nothing of Myself; but as My Father taught Me, I speak these things. And He who sent Me is with Me. The Father has not left Me alone, for I always do those things that please Him." As He spoke these words, many believed in Him. (John 8:23–30 NKJV)

Jesus makes this statement very clear. He did nothing of His own accord or by His own choice or by His own authority, but only as the Father taught Him. He was always in complete agreement with the Father. Jesus was one with the Father. He never sought His own will. He was completely occupied with what His Father was saying and doing. His heart and mind were focused on His Father. Many times throughout the gospels, He states that He only did what He saw the Father do and He only said what He heard the Father say. He was in perfect harmony and unity with His Father, and in this way, He honored His Father. Most importantly, take notice that He said the Father had not left Him alone, for Jesus always did the things that pleased Him, namely what He had just heard or seen from the Father! That is to say, Jesus abided in the words of His Father!

> Then Jesus said to those Jews who believed Him, "If you abide in My word, you are My disciples indeed. And you shall know the truth, and the truth shall make you free." (John 8:31–32 NKJV)

Wow! He gives them a great revelation. "If you abide in My words, you shall know the truth, and by knowing the truth, you will be made free!" The word *abide* means to live, or to remain. But it also means to continue in a particular condition, attitude, or relationship. He is telling them that if they receive His teaching, they will be set free because His teaching is truth. Unfortunately, the Pharisees could not abide in Jesus's words because they were not open to receive from Him. His words had no place in their hearts.

> They answered Him, "We are Abraham's descendants, and have never been in bondage to anyone. How can You say, 'You will be made free'?" Jesus answered them, "Most assuredly, I say to you, whoever commits sin is a slave of sin. And a slave does not abide in the house forever, but a son abides

> forever. Therefore if the Son makes you free, you
> shall be free indeed. (John 8:33–36 NKJV)

Wow! Again another amazing statement made by Jesus. He is saying that as the Son of God, He abides forever, and because He sets us free, we are truly free. Jesus did not condemn the guilty but said, "Follow Me and you will not walk in the dark, in what is false, but you will have the light, which is life. And you will *know* the truth and the truth will set you free. Your eyes will be opened to know truth."

> "I know that you are Abraham's descendants, but
> you seek to kill Me, because My word has no place
> in you. I speak what I have seen with My Father,
> and you do what you have seen with your father."
> (John 8:37–38 NKJV)

I love His boldness! Notice also that Jesus said His word had no place in them. In other words, His word could not abide in them. It could not live or remain in them because they refused to believe it. Again, He only spoke what He heard from the Father. It is so clear that everything Jesus did or said was exactly what He received from God. He was always in perfect agreement with the Father because He knew that whatever God said or did was truth. This is the beautiful picture of the love and trust between the Father and the Son. It didn't matter that these religious leaders were out to kill Jesus. He was secure in the love of His Father.

> They answered and said to Him, "Abraham is our
> father." Jesus said to them, "If you were Abraham's
> children, you would do the works of Abraham. But
> now you seek to kill Me, a Man who has told you
> the truth which I heard from God. (John 8:39–40
> NKJV)

Did you get that? The words that Jesus just told them were words of truth He heard from God. Receiving God's word is everything because our faith comes by hearing the word of God. Receiving God's word is vital because it is truth. Consequently, receiving anything contrary would be a lie, and believing a lie is what started the whole mess in the first place! As I said before, it takes a humble heart to receive the word of God.

In Mark chapter 4 Jesus began to teach about the necessity of hearing God's word and receiving it as truth. The Bible says He was before a great crowd of people along the lakeside of the Sea of Galilee. He started out by saying, "Pay attention" to this parable because if you do not understand this parable, you won't be able to understand all other parables. In other words, all other parables would hinge on their ability to comprehend this parable. It was foundational. Many people are familiar with Jesus's teaching of the sower. He explains that the sower goes out to sow. First the seed falls on the path, where the birds eat it up. Next the seed falls on ground full of rocks, and because it cannot take root, it withers away. Then the seed is sown among thorns and thistles so it becomes suffocated and does not yield much fruit. Finally, the seed falls on good soil, where it produces grain, some thirty times, some sixty times, and some even one hundred times as much as had been sown.

In verse 10 we find that as soon as Jesus was alone, the twelve disciples and those who were closest to Him began to ask the meaning of the parable. Jesus said the mystery of the kingdom of God is about to be revealed to them, because the secret counsels of God are hidden, but only to those who have no desire to know. God reveals truth to those who seek to know. That's why the passage said the twelve disciples and those who were closest to Him. If you have the desire to know God, you will find Him.

Jesus proceeds to reveal the mystery of the Kingdom of God by explaining the meaning of the sower and the seed. The seed is the Word of God. The soil that receives the seed is represented by four people groups. Or specifically, we can say four kinds of hearts. First, when the seed is sown along the path, which represents hard soil, the people hear the word being taught, but the enemy comes at once and takes the message out of their hearts. In other words, the heart does not receive the word. The seed sown on stony ground represents those who hear the word but have no real root or foundation of truth in them to allow the word to grow and produce fruit. The seed sown among the thorns is reflective of the cares and distractions of this world, which cause people to take their eyes off the word, and consequently, there is no fruit produced in their lives. Finally, the seed sown in good soil represents the hearts of people who receive and accept the word of God and allow that truth to be planted deep in their hearts, where it begins to bear fruit, some thirty, some sixty, and some one hundred times as much as was sown.

Then Jesus continues to explain how the Kingdom of God operates by giving a similar parable.

> And he said, So is the kingdom of God, as if a man should cast seed into the ground; And should sleep, and rise night and day, and the seed should spring and grow up, he knoweth not how. For the earth bringeth forth fruit of herself; first the blade, then the ear, after that the full corn in the ear. But when the fruit is brought forth, immediately he putteth in the sickle, because the harvest is come. (Mark 4:26–29 KJV)

He explains that the kingdom is like a man scattering seed and sleeping night and day while the seed begins to work in the ground. The reason a farmer can sleep night and day is because he knows the seed is working. He has taken the time to prepare the soil so the conditions are just right to cause the seed to bring forth the best harvest. The farmer doesn't wonder if it will produce, but He waits patiently because he knows that in time that seed will begin to germinate and sprout, and without fail, it will produce the crop specific to that particular seed.

Verse 28 says the earth produces by itself, first the blade, then the ear, then the full grain in the ear. Now think of this verse in light of the fact that Jesus is explaining how the kingdom of God operates. First of all, the earth produces by itself. The earth in this sense is talking about our hearts or the soil of our hearts. Remember, God does not force anyone to believe Him. He has given us free will to choose as we like. Our hearts can choose to hear the Word of God and receive the truth of the Bible or not. The heart produces by itself. We have free will. Secondly, recognize the progression of the word planted in our hearts. The verse says first the blade, which represents the beginning of growth. Then the ear is produced, which is the beginning of fruit, and finally the full grain in the ear, which represents a full harvest. Now Jesus said the seed sown in the good soil, or heart, would produce fruit at three different levels, thirty, sixty, and one hundred times.

Let's look at the progression of the blade, the ear and the full corn in the ear according to Vines Expository Dictionary. The word "blade" is the Greek word, *chortos*, and it means grass, a feeding enclosure or my personal favorite, a garden. God's word is food. The Bible tells us that man shall not live by bread alone but by every word that proceeds out of the mouth of God, Deuteronomy 8:3. This is a profound truth that we must understand and put into practice as believers. The Word of God is food, and just as our bodies need food to be properly nourished to be healthy and strong, so also our spirits, our true natures, must receive the word of God into our hearts as food.

The word *ear* is the Greek word *stathus*. It is derived from the root sta-, which means "to cause to stand." As we begin to receive God's word into our hearts and allow it to take root so we become established in our thinking, the word causes us to stand. It causes us to be firm in our beliefs. We stand fixed on the truth of God's word.

Finally, the third stage is the full corn in the ear, which signifies the sense of being complete or having full measure. Jesus is saying that as we receive the word of God into our hearts and allow it to mature, it will produce fruit one hundred times over. The key is allowing it to produce.

Hebrews chapter 11 is known as the great hall of faith. Verse 1 tell us that faith is the substance of things hoped for, the evidence of things not seen. The word *substance* is the Greek word *hypostasis*, and it means a substructure or foundation. Our faith gives us confidence because it is secure on the foundation of who God truly is for us. When the Bible talks about hope, it is not like the hope of the world that says, "Well, let's just hope so." No, Bible hope is a positive expectation of good. That's why faith and hope are tied together. We can stand on a firm foundation of God's word to us with a positive expectation of good. That is faith, and that is what pleases God. When that seed is in the ground, the farmer has faith that it is working. In the same way, the word of God is alive, and it will produce if we allow it to take root and develop.

> For as the rain and snow come down from the heavens, and return not there again, but water the earth and make it bring forth and sprout, that it may give seed to the sower and bread to the eater, So shall My word be that goes forth out of My mouth: it shall not return to Me void [without producing any effect, useless], but it shall accomplish that which I please and purpose, and it shall prosper

in the thing for which I sent it. (Isaiah 55:10–11 AMPC)

God's word will not return void. It will produce. Hebrews 4:12 tells us that the word of God is alive and active. It is full of power. When God spoke, things were created. I love the way the Amplified Bible speaks of God's word in Colossians 1:5–6:

> Of this [hope] you heard in the past in the message
> of the truth of the Gospel, which has come to you.
> Indeed, in the whole world [that Gospel] is bearing
> fruit and still is growing [by its own inherent power].

The gospel is the message of salvation through Christ, and that message, that word is producing and growing by its own power. Inherent means existing in someone or something as a permanent and inseparable element, quality, or attribute. That's why the word is called a seed. It has the ability within itself to produce!

Now because we live in a fallen world, our faith will be tested. James chapter 1 says the proving of our faith will bring out patience, but let patience do a thorough work so you may be perfectly mature.

> Be assured and understand that the trial and proving
> of your faith bring out endurance and steadfastness
> and patience. But let endurance and steadfastness
> and patience have full play and do a thorough work,
> so that you may be [people] perfectly and fully
> developed [with no defects], lacking in nothing.
> (James 1:3–4 AMPC)

Wow that's quite a promise. If we will continue to trust God in the difficult times, it will develop our character to such a degree that we will lack nothing. This is where we learn to rely on God in complete surrender to His love and goodness toward us.

Notice this is how the apostle Paul explains the message of the gospel of Christ.

> For I am not ashamed of the Gospel (good news) of Christ, for it is God's power working unto salvation [for deliverance from eternal death] to everyone who believes with a personal trust and a confident surrender and firm reliance, to the Jew first and also to the Greek. (Romans 1:16 AMPC)

The power of God is in the message of salvation through Christ. It's the power of God's word working in believers. Believing is the key. We choose to believe that what God says is the truth. We choose to believe regardless of anything that is contrary. I love how the Amplified says a personal trust, a confident surrender, and a firm reliance. That speaks of intimacy. That speaks of our relationship with our Creator. We take God at His word because we trust Him and know that He is good. We know that He accepts us, approves us, and is well pleased with us!

The word of God is powerful and alive because it is the truth. We must believe and receive the truth and allow it to be planted within our hearts. When we do this, it cannot help but produce life—true life within us.

When the farmer plants a seed, it must be planted down into the soil, where it is unseen. In the same way, faith is the unseen realm. We know from Hebrews 11 that faith is a substance that works in the unseen realm.

> Now faith is the substance of things hoped for, the
> evidence of things not seen. (Hebrews 11:1 NKJV)

Since faith is a substance, that means there's something to it. It may not be tangible, but in the spirit realm it has substance. Just like the seed in the soil is unseen, so our faith may not be seen, but it has substance. There is weightiness to it. So just like that seed in the ground, you wait on it. You allow it to germinate. You allow it to take root. A farmer doesn't go out and dig up the seed to see if it is growing. He doesn't wonder if it's beginning to take root and starting to grow. No, the farmer is patient, the Bible says. He believes the seed he planted will take root. He expects a harvest from that seed, so he waits patiently. He rests in the fact that he knows that seed will produce exactly what it is designed to produce. Faith is the substance of things hoped for. Hope means a positive expectation of good. The substance of faith is a positive expectation of good.

Habakkuk 2:3 says though it tarry, wait, for it shall surely come. Wait. Even when it takes more time than you think it should, wait. You trust God and rest in Him, knowing that He is faithful and His word is working. As you patiently wait, you are allowing that substance to have deep roots. Though it tarry, wait, for it will surely come to pass. It will come forth on its appointed day. There is an appointed day.

The vision is for an appointed time. That seed will produce the harvest it was designed to produce.

> In the beginning [before all time] was the *Word* (Christ), and the *Word* was with God, and the *Word* was God Himself. (John 1:1 AMPC)

> And the *Word* (Christ) became flesh (human, incarnate) and tabernacled (fixed His tent of flesh, lived awhile) among us; and

we [actually] saw His glory (His honor, His majesty), such glory as an only begotten son receives from his father, full of grace (favor, loving-kindness) and truth. (John 1:14 AMPC)

Christ is the word of God. He is the word of truth planted in our hearts.

WE LIVE WHAT WE BELIEVE

The Bible tells us in Proverbs 23:7 that as a man thinks in his heart, so is he. In other words, what we believe will be displayed in our behavior, in our actions, and in our attitudes. The way we think will manifest itself throughout our lives. This tells us there is great power in the way we think. At the new birth, our spirit man was completely reborn and we became a new creation. Our spirit man was quickened or made alive. However, our soul, which is made up of our mind, our will, and our emotions, was not the part of man that was made new. This is extremely vital to understand to live out of our new nature. In fact, the thoughts of man are so powerful that God gives evidence to this in Genesis 11 when the people wanted to build the tower of Babel.

In chapter 1, we find that the whole earth was of one language and of one speech. The people at that time had journeyed to the region of Babylonia and dwelt in a place called Shinar. There the people decided to build a city with a tower whose top would reach the heavens. The interesting thing about this is that God came down to see their city and tower and said,

> "Indeed the people are one and they all have one language, and this is what they begin to do; now nothing that they propose to do will be withheld from them. Come, let Us go down and there confuse

their language, that they may not understand one
another's speech." (Genesis 11:6-7 NKJV)

When it says they were of one language, it means they were of
one mind. They were in agreement. They thought alike, and they
spoke alike. There was no disagreement. Their thoughts were in
agreement, so consequently their actions were unlimited. God said
nothing they purposed to do would be withheld from them. They
were united in thought so they could accomplish whatever they
purposed to do. This is remarkable when you realize the magnitude
of what God was saying. It has to do with the power of unity, the
power of agreement.

So how does this apply to us today as believers? When we renew
our minds to the word of God, the Bible says we are transformed
into knowing what is the good, acceptable, and perfect will of God.

> And do not be conformed to this world, but be
> transformed by the renewing of your mind, that
> you may prove what is that good and acceptable and
> perfect will of God. (Romans 12:2 NKJV)

Be constantly renewed in the spirit of your mind. We are a new spirit,
but the thoughts of our mind must be renewed to agree with our
new spirit. It has everything to do with how we think. We tend to
think in agreement with our old nature, so when things happen and
situations come up in life, we revert back to our old way of thinking.
The word says one thing, but our reasoning says something quite
different. We try and justify or give reasons for what we believe to be
right, even though it's contrary to what God says. We will continue
to do this until our minds are renewed to think differently. We are
never going to change our actions until we change the way we think
about some things. The gospel is not about changing our behavior.
Our behavior will begin to change automatically when we begin to

think differently. Jesus is the truth. There is the truth. There are not many truths in the world. Since God is truth, what He says is true, and we need to begin to think like Him. We have to change the way we think. We have to know what He would be thinking in the situation. Our minds are going to want to reason it away. Our minds are going to want to talk us out of it. That's exactly what the enemy did to Jesus after He was baptized and led into the wilderness. Satan tried to change His thinking. He didn't threaten to kill Jesus. Instead he tempted Jesus in His thinking. He tried to cause Him to second guess God. Jesus had just been told by God, "You are My beloved Son in whom I am well pleased." Jesus knew who He was, and He knew how His Father thought of Him. The enemy came along and tried to get Him to think differently about himself and about His relationship with God.

> The tempter came to him and said, "If you are the Son of God, tell these stones to become bread."
> (Matthew 4:3 NIV)

That's what the enemy does with us. He tries to get us to think differently. He tries to get us to revert to old ways of looking at things. God says one thing, but our mind says a completely different thing.

The mind of Christ is the most amazing thing ever, and 1 Corinthians 2:16 tells us we have the mind of Christ. We can know His thoughts through the word and through the indwelling Holy Spirit. We are transformed by the renewing of our minds so we may know the good, acceptable, and perfect will of God. We must know the truth of what God says about us, because as a man thinks in his heart, so is he.

Remember, the spirit of man has come alive to God, but our soul, which is our mind, will, and emotions, needs to be taught the word of God. That's where the word *repent* comes in. The Greek word is *metanoia,* which means a change of mind. The kingdom of God operates in a completely different way than what we are accustomed to, so we have to change the way we think about things to receive the Word of God. All the miracles, signs, and wonders that Jesus performed while on earth were not accomplished because He was deity. The miracles were accomplished because He operated by the laws of the Kingdom of God. He defied the laws that govern this physical realm because He operated by the principles of the Kingdom, the spiritual realm, which are greater than this physical realm because the spiritual created the physical. The bottom line is that we must receive the word of God as truth and renew our minds to it. We need to think like God thinks. We make the choice to believe His word. Remember, Jesus was in perfect agreement with the Father.

In 2 Corinthians chapter 3, we are told that as we behold as in a mirror the glory of the Lord, we are changed from glory to glory. Christ is the Word, so as we read the word and receive the truth about whom our Creator really is and what He says about us and this life, we are changed into His very image from glory to glory. Our minds begin to be renewed to think like God. Our minds begin to be renewed to believe like God. As a man thinks in his heart, so is he. As our minds are renewed to think like God, we then come into agreement with Him. We come into unity with Him.

This is exactly what Jesus was saying in John 17 just before He went to the cross. He prayed to the Father that believers would become one just as He and the Father are one. To be one with someone is to be in agreement with him or her, as we just read about when the Israelites wanted to build the tower to heaven. God said nothing they agreed to do would be withheld from them because they were of one mind. They were in perfect agreement. They were one. Now as believers in Christ we have become one with Him and with each other.

We know from Genesis that Adam was not faithful. He doubted what God had told him. He allowed the lie of the devil to question the truth of what God had said. But Christ was faithful. We find in Hebrews 3 that Jesus was faithful over his Father's house as a Son.

> But Christ was faithful as a Son over His house—whose house we are, if we hold fast our confidence and the boast of our hope firm until the end. (Hebrews 3:6 NASB)

Now we are members of God's house, His Kingdom, as sons and daughters because of our placement in Christ. As sons and daughters, we remain faithful to God. But this faithfulness is not about doing all the right things. Remember, we are given the gift of righteousness because of our believing, not by our works. So we continue to stand righteous before God and remain faithful by believing in the finished work of Christ. In Hebrews 3 the writer goes on to say that the Holy Spirit says, "Today, if you will hear His voice do not harden your hearts as Israel did in the day of testing in the wilderness."

> Therefore, as the Holy Spirit says: "Today, if you will hear His voice, Do not harden your hearts as in the rebellion, in the day of trial in the wilderness, where your fathers tested Me, tried Me, and saw My works forty years." (Hebrews 3:7–9 NKJV)

The Israelites had been in bondage for four hundred years when God supernaturally brought them out of Egypt. From the ten plagues against the Egyptians, to the parting of the Red Sea, to a daily provision of food in the desert for more than 2 million people, the Israelites had experienced a tremendous deliverance, yet they murmured and complained and even begged Moses to take them back to Egypt. This new freedom was a complete reversal of their former existence. As slaves they were downcast, broke, sick, helpless, and hopeless. Then suddenly they were marched out of Egypt healthy, strong, and rich. Their life had radically changed. Their existence as slaves ended, but their mentality as slaves remained. They could not adjust to their newfound freedom and their new identity. Their deliverance is a type or shadow, a picture of the freedom we obtain when we receive Christ. We become sons and daughters and are set free from the bondage of slavery, namely the bondage of sin we were born into. In the same way, as believers in Christ, we are a new creation with a new spirit. However, our minds must be renewed to our new existence and our new identity.

The main point I want to make about this passage in Hebrews 3 is the mention of a hardened heart. In regard to the Israelites, the Holy Spirit said that generation always erred and was led astray in their hearts. When the Bible talks about a hardened heart, it's actually talking about an unbelieving heart. And because it is unbelieving, God considers it wicked, sinful, and evil. A hardened heart is a heart of unbelief.

> Beware, brethren, lest there be in any of you an evil heart of unbelief in departing from the living God. (Hebrews 3:12 NKJV)

> See to it, brothers and sisters, that none of you has a sinful, unbelieving heart that turns away from the living God. (Hebrews 3:12 NIV)

> [Therefore beware] brethren, take care, lest there be in any one of you a wicked, unbelieving heart [which refuses to cleave to, trust in, and rely on

> Him], leading you to turn away and desert or stand
> aloof from the living God. (Hebrews 3:12 AMPC)

Having faith and believing in God and His word is the foundation of Christianity. Our faith pleases God because we believe He exists and it honors Him when we trust that what He says is true. Again, it's about a relationship that's built on trust. The heart of man is where we believe. You can believe something with your mind, but when it drops into your heart, it becomes rooted and established into the person you are. The heart reveals the inner character of a person. As a man thinks in his heart, so is he. What you believe in your heart reveals your character, and it's what comes out of your mouth. What we believe in our hearts, we speak. Jesus said it this way. Out of the abundance of the heart, the mouth speaks. At one time the Pharisees questioned Jesus as to why His disciples didn't wash their hands before eating, as was one of their many ceremonial traditions. They accused the disciples of being unclean, but Jesus said it's not what goes into a man that makes him unclean but rather what comes out. What is in your heart will eventually come out.

> Therefore, as the Holy Spirit says: "Today, if you
> will hear His voice, Do not harden your hearts as
> in the rebellion, in the day of trial in the wilderness,
> where your fathers tested Me, tried Me, and saw
> My works forty years. Therefore I was angry with
> that generation, and said, 'They always go astray in
> their heart, and they have not known My ways.' So I
> swore in My wrath, 'They shall not enter My rest.'"
> (Hebrews 3:7–11 NJKV)

In verse 10, the Holy Spirit said the Israelites did not perceive or recognize or know God's ways. The transformation necessary for them to stay out of Egypt, out of bondage, was the renewing of their minds from a slave mentality to a sonship mentality. God was their provider, protector, and deliverer. He had already shown them over and over, but they continued to doubt. Their identity was still rooted in slavery. Consider this in light of the truth that we have received righteousness, right standing with God, and have been placed into Christ because of God's great love and desire to be in relationship with us. That is God's way today. He is well pleased with us. He has placed us into His Beloved. Our hearts need to receive that and not go astray from that truth. I love how the Holy Spirit says, "Today if you will hear His voice." It is a daily reminder for us to receive the truth of how God really sees and feels about us every day.

> Take care, brothers, lest there be in any of you an evil, unbelieving heart, leading you to fall away from the living God. (Hebrews 3:12 ESV)

Verse 12 describes an evil or wicked heart as being an unbelieving heart that refuses to trust and rely on God. This unbelief causes the heart to turn away from and even desert the living God. The writer of Hebrews warns against this and admonishes instead to hold fast to the confidence and trust in the finished work of Christ. A wicked heart is simply a heart that refuses to trust God. I believe trust is the greatest honor we can give to God. It is an acknowledgment that He is a loving Creator. Let's face it—how can you have faith in someone unless you trust him or her. I believe that is why faith pleases God. Faith says, "I trust that what you say is true." God loves us, and He is well pleased with us. That is truth. That is the right perspective we must have of God.

Notice verse 11 says that because their hearts were unbelieving, they would not enter into rest. This is essential for us as believers. The writer of Hebrews goes on to say that the promise of entering into rest still holds true for us today. We rest in the finished work of Christ. We rest in the truth that God is pleased with us. We rest in the truth that God sees us in His precious Son. We rest in the truth that we partake of all that Christ accomplished for us. Remember, that's why God placed us into Christ. We enter into rest when we believe!

> For indeed the gospel was preached to us as well as to them; but the word which they heard did not profit them, not being mixed with faith in those who heard it. For we who have believed do enter that rest, as He has said: "So I swore in My wrath, 'They shall not enter My rest, although the works were finished from the foundation of the world. (Hebrews 4:2-3 NKJV)

The writer continues by stating that the Israelites were given the good news that they were to enter into the Promised Land. However, they did not enter because of disobedience! God equates unbelief with disobedience. Remember, He calls an unbelieving heart a wicked, evil and sinful heart. Unbelief is actually the greatest sin of all. On the other hand, when we believe and put our faith in God, it honors Him and brings us into agreement with Him.

> Seeing then that the promise remains over [from past times] for some to enter that rest, and that those who formerly were given the good news about it and the opportunity, failed to appropriate it and did not enter because of disobedience. (Hebrews 3:6 AMPC)

Faith is a rest. If we are unrestful, we are simply not in faith. We continue to hear the word of God because faith comes by hearing God's word, and we choose to believe it regardless of circumstances. By doing so, we are being obedient and are honoring God.

> Again He designates a certain day, saying in David, "Today," after such a long time, as it has been said: "Today, if you will hear His voice, Do not harden your hearts." For if Joshua had given them rest, then He would not afterward have spoken of another day. There remains therefore a rest for the people of God. For he who has entered His rest has himself also ceased from his works as God did from His. Let us therefore be diligent to enter that rest, lest anyone fall according to the same example of disobedience. (Hebrews 3:7–11 NKJV)

Notice verse 10 says that we can know we have entered into rest because we have stopped trying to work things out on our own. Rest can become a gauge for us to determine whether we are actually in faith. If we are restless, then we are not in faith. Faith is a rest. What a remarkable freedom the Lord has given to us! The world today is restless in so many ways. It is said that stress is a predominant reason why many people are sick and weary in their bodies and minds. To be able to live with peace of mind in a world full of turmoil is an amazing gift. That's why this verse says we must strive to enter into this rest.

> For he who has once entered [God's] rest also has ceased from [the weariness and pain] of human labors, just as God rested from those labors peculiarly His own. Let us therefore be zealous and exert ourselves and strive diligently to enter that rest [of God, to know and experience it for ourselves], that no one may fall or perish by the same kind of unbelief and disobedience [into which those in the wilderness fell]. (Hebrews 3:10–11 AMPC)

The world will constantly try to pull us into unrest. But thanks to God, Christ is our peace. Our relationship with God must be based on trust, and then we can enter into true rest. When we are in rest, our perspective is correct. The right perspective will always give us rest.

We find a wonderful promise in the book of Isaiah.

> You will keep him in perfect peace, whose mind is stayed on You, Because he trusts in You. (Isaiah 26:3 NKJV)

I've heard this verse quoted many times, but usually the last part is omitted. People will say that God will keep you in peace if you keep your mind on Him. However, the verse is telling us that if we keep our thoughts on God, then He will keep us in perfect peace *because* we trust in Him. Now if we have an incorrect view of what God's thoughts are about us, then we cannot possibly keep our minds focused on trusting Him. If we do not trust that God loves and accepts and approves of us and that He is well pleased with us, then we cannot be in perfect peace. If our perspective about the truth of God's heart toward us is false in any area of our lives, we cannot possibly have a peaceful mind that trusts in Him. It is imperative that we know the truth about God's heart toward us. He sees us in Christ. He sees us in the perfection of His Son. We are clothed with Christ. We are accepted in the Beloved. God does not change about how He sees us. We are in Christ, and God is well pleased with us. That does not change because God does not change. Remember, He reconciled us to Himself through Christ because of His great love. His love, acceptance, and approval toward us are not based on what we have or have not done. Our relationship must be based on the finished work of Christ. We remain faithful because He is faithful and true. So when our minds agree with the truth of who God is toward us, then and only then will our minds be trusting toward Him and the perfect peace will come.

We find in the gospels that after Jesus was baptized by John, many people began to go to Jesus to be baptized instead of going to John. Some were upset by this and questioned John about it. He responded by saying that he must decrease, while Jesus must increase. John had no doubts about who Jesus was at this point, and he continued by encouraging the people to listen and follow Jesus.

> He Who comes from above (heaven) is [far] above all [others]; he who comes from the earth belongs to the earth, and talks the language of earth [his words are from an earthly standpoint]. He Who comes from heaven is [far] above all others [far superior to all others in prominence and in excellence]. It is to what He has [actually] seen and heard that He bears testimony, and yet no one accepts His testimony [no one receives His evidence as true]. Whoever receives His testimony has set his seal of approval to this: God is true. [That man has definitely certified, acknowledged, declared once and for all, and is himself assured that it is divine truth that God cannot lie]. For since He Whom God has sent speaks the words of God [proclaims God's own message], God does not give Him His Spirit sparingly or by measure, but boundless is the gift God makes of His Spirit! The Father loves the Son and has given (entrusted, committed) everything into His hand. And he who believes in (has faith in, clings to, relies on) the Son has (now possesses) eternal life. But whoever disobeys (is unbelieving toward, refuses to trust in, disregards, is not subject to) the Son will never see (experience) life, but [instead] the wrath of

God abides on him. [God's displeasure remains on him; His indignation hangs over him continually.] (John 3:31–36 AMPC)

Notice that verse 36 says that those who are unbelieving toward and refuse to trust in the Son, will never see or experience life. This is a profound statement because it confirms the truth that until a person is born again, he or she cannot experience life. Their spirit is not actually alive. The sin nature still exists, and since the wages of sin is death, they cannot experience the life that only Christ can give. The gift of righteousness through Christ gives life—true life.

> Yes, Adam's one sin brings condemnation for everyone, but Christ's one act of righteousness brings a right relationship with God and new life for everyone. (Romans 5:18 NLT)

A NEW PERSPECTIVE IN CHRIST

In John 16 the disciples asked Jesus to show them the Father. His response was, "What? Have I been with you for so long and you still not understand? If you've seen me, you've seen the Father." Jesus and the Father are one, and as already stated, everything Jesus did or said was in complete agreement and harmony with the Father.

If we want to know what God is like, we look to Jesus because He is the exact representation of the Father, as we read in Hebrews 1:3:

> He is the sole expression of the glory of God [the Light-being, the out-raying or radiance of the divine], and He is the perfect imprint and very image of [God's] nature, upholding and maintaining and guiding and propelling the universe by His mighty word of power. When He had by offering Himself accomplished our cleansing of sins and riddance of guilt, He sat down at the right hand of the divine Majesty on high. (AMPC)

In chapter 1, the writer of Hebrews continues by saying that man was given revelation of the truth through the word of the prophets. But in these last days, God has spoken to us through His Son, Jesus Christ. There are over 330 prophecies in the Old Testament that specifically foretell the coming of Christ Jesus. And as amazing as it may seem, it is still no surprise that in only three and half years, Jesus fulfilled every one of those prophecies. Shortly before Jesus began His ministry, John the Baptist appeared in the wilderness, crying out to the people to prepare the way of the Lord. Speaking of John the Baptist, the prophet Isaiah wrote, "I will send My messenger before Your face, who will make ready Your way." John told the people, "He's coming! Get ready!" John preached repentance, which means to change the way you think, for the kingdom is heaven is at hand. The kingdom of God is about to show up in this earth. The kingdom of God is about to be displayed and revealed in this earthly kingdom. So Jesus began His ministry preaching the good news of the gospel of the kingdom of God! The gospel is the message that Christ preached and taught. The gospel is the good news that God sent His Son to die for the sins of mankind and give them eternal life. I love the way Matthew 1:21 says it in the Amplified Bible:

> She will bear a Son, and you shall call His name Jesus [the Greek form of the Hebrew Joshua, which means Savior], for He will save His people from their sins [that is, prevent them from failing and missing the true end and scope of life, which is God].

Living a life without knowing God is absolutely the most tragic thing there is. Remember, the meaning of sin is to miss the mark. God is the mark. He is life and the life giver. God is the true meaning to life. Eternal life is to know God. When you know God, you know truth.

So Jesus came preaching the message of the kingdom of God. But He said to understand the kingdom of God, you'll have to repent. You'll have to change the way you think because the kingdom of God operates unlike anything you've ever seen or heard of before. You'll have to change your perspective. Not only did Jesus teach about the kingdom, but He revealed the kingdom. While ministering to crowds throughout Israel for three years, Jesus healed the sick, raised the dead, opened blind eyes, multiplied food, walked on water, and delivered and set people free. He displayed the kingdom of God with signs, wonders, and miracles that astonished all who beheld His glory and power. Remember, He said, "If you've seen Me, you've seen the Father." He displayed the heart of God!

Now as believers in Christ we have been placed into the kingdom of God. The Bible says we are in this world, but we are not of this world.

> [The Father] has delivered and drawn us to Himself
> out of the control and the dominion of darkness and
> has transferred us into the kingdom of the Son of
> His love. (Colossians 1:13 AMPC)

Now our new life must operate according to the kingdom of God. In Genesis 2 we read that after Adam and Eve ate from the tree of the knowledge of good and evil, they were afraid, and they hid themselves because their entire perspective had changed. Then God asked them three very important questions. The first question God asked was, "Where are you?" That is the same question we must ask ourselves today. If our perspective is correct and we ask ourselves, "Where are we?" our answer should be that we are seated with Christ in heavenly places. We are in Christ. We are in a position of royalty, dignity, honor, and majesty because we are in Christ. That's where we truly are. Our perspective of how we view life on a daily basis needs to be from our position of being in Christ. However, if we do not have a revelation of this truth and we are not renewed in our minds to this truth, then we will view our lives with limitations from a much lower perspective.

The second question God asked Adam was, "Who told you that you were naked?" We must ask ourselves, "Who are we listening to?" If our perspective is correct, we will recognize the voice of the enemy. He is called the accuser of the brethren. If our thoughts are condemning, critical, or accusing us in any way, then we must cast those thoughts down. They are not from God the Father, who loves us and sent His Beloved Son to die for our sins. Jesus paid the highest price. He gave His very life. Jesus said He came to save man, not to condemn man.

> For God did not send the Son into the world in order
> to judge (to reject, to condemn, to pass sentence on)
> the world, but that the world might find salvation
> and be made safe and sound through Him. (John
> 3:17 AMPC)

It would be a dishonor to all that Christ did for mankind to think that God would condemn a man for his shortcomings after he has been placed into Christ. Jesus did not die in vain. He said, "It is finished," and we need to understand that His death provided an everlasting release for all of mankind, whether they receive it or not. Do not believe the lies of the enemy! Romans 8:1–4 tells us:

> There is therefore now no condemnation to those
> who are in Christ Jesus, who do not walk according
> to the flesh, but according to the Spirit. For the law
> of the Spirit of life in Christ Jesus has made me free
> from the law of sin and death. For what the law
> could not do in that it was weak through the flesh,
> God did by sending His own Son in the likeness of
> sinful flesh, on account of sin: He condemned sin in
> the flesh, that the righteous requirement of the law
> might be fulfilled in us who do not walk according
> to the flesh but according to the Spirit. (NKJV)

We are not who we used to be. The Bible says we were crucified with Christ. Our sin nature died when Christ died. We were raised up when Christ was raised up. We recognize that Jesus's death was our death and that sin in our flesh was defeated in Christ's body on the cross. We are regenerated spirit beings who are led by the Holy Spirit within.

That's why there is therefore no condemnation for those who are in Christ Jesus, for the law of the Spirit of life in Christ Jesus has made us free from the law of sin and death.

The third question God asked Adam was, "Have you eaten from the tree that I commanded you not to eat from?" In other words, what are you partaking of? Where are you getting your nourishment from? What are you participating with? What are you engaging with? What are you receiving from? We must ask ourselves the same questions. As new creations in Christ, we receive all Christ is for us. Jesus lived out of His relationship with His Father, and now we live out our relationship with Christ. We live in Christ, we live by or because of Christ, we live through Christ, and He lives through us. This is how Jesus described His union with the Father and our union with Him.

> Just as the living Father sent Me and I live by (through, because of) the Father, even so whoever continues to feed on Me [whoever takes Me for his food and is nourished by Me] shall [in his turn] live through and because of Me. (John 6:57 AMPC)

Recognize the relationship of Jesus to the Father! Our lives are to be lived in the same manner, completely dependent on Christ, yielding to His life within.

In 2 Corinthians 4, we are given an amazing statement.

> For it is the God who commanded light to shine out of darkness, who has shone in our hearts to give the light of the knowledge of the glory of God in the face of Jesus Christ. (2 Corinthians 4:6 NKJV)

> For God Who said, Let light shine out of darkness, has shone in our hearts so as [to beam forth] the Light for the illumination of the knowledge of the majesty and glory of God [as it is manifest in the Person and is revealed] in the face of Jesus Christ (the Messiah). (2 Corinthians 4:6 AMPC)

The word *light* is used twice in this verse, and each has a different Hebrew meaning. The first use of the word is referring to the "light" God spoke in Genesis 1:3. This is the first reference of God speaking when He said, "Let there be light." The light He spoke of is the Hebrew word *owr*, which means the opposite of darkness. Verse 2 tells us that there was darkness over the face of the deep, and when God said, "Let there be light," he separated darkness from light. We know that this light was not the light of the created sun because later in verse 16, God created two bodies of light, the sun and the moon and the stars also. This word for light in the Hebrew is *maor*, which denotes a luminary body.

Second Corinthians 4:6 goes on to say that the light God first spoke is like the light He has shone in our hearts. This second use of the word *light* is the Greek word *photismos*, which means to shine, to make illuminated, to give light as reaching the mind. It other words, this light brings understanding to the mind. The verse continues by saying that the light that is shone in our hearts is to give illumination to the knowledge of the glory of God in the face of Jesus. There is so much packed into this one verse!

It has to do with knowledge, revelation knowledge of who we are in Christ. As a man thinks in his heart, so is he. God gave the light for the knowledge of the glory of God in the face of Jesus. Eternal life is to know God. It's heart knowledge. It's knowledge of God's goodness toward us. It's knowledge of the love that has been shed abroad in our hearts by the Holy Spirit who has been given to us. It's knowledge of Christ within, the hope of realizing the glory. It's the hope of realizing how good God is. The hope of realizing how God sees us, feels about us, and thinks of us. It's His opinion of us. He has given us glory, which means He has a good opinion of us, and it results in honor, glory, and dignity!

Before we are born again, the Bible says mankind is in darkness, meaning that man does not understand the truth. Man does not see clearly. We know this to be true, as was stated earlier when talking about Adam and the change in his perspective when he did what God told him not to do. When he chose not to trust God but instead made his own decision, his entire view of life was darkened. He lost the ability to comprehend or to understand the things of the spirit. We know this also according to 1 Corinthians 2:14, which states that the natural or nonspiritual man cannot know or receive the things of the spirit because they are spiritually discerned. The "light" or understanding and comprehension of the truth have not entered into the heart of a nonbeliever. The light that God spoke to separate the darkness is the same light that He now shines in our hearts to bring us revelation, understanding, and knowledge of the truth of God in the face of Jesus!

Second Corinthians 4:4 explains it this way:

> For the god of this world has blinded the unbelievers' minds [that they should not discern the truth], preventing them from seeing the illuminating light

of the Gospel of the glory of Christ (the Messiah),
Who is the Image and Likeness of God. (AMPC)

Blinded in this sense means a dulled spiritual perception and
hardness of the heart. What happened in the garden of Eden when
Adam ate the fruit caused his entire perception of how he viewed
God and himself to darken. His perception was dulled, and his heart
or we can say his understanding was hardened to truth.

The meaning of the word *mind* in this verse is the Greek word
noema, and it means mental perception. The god of this world
has darkened the mental perception of the unbelieving man. This
same word *noema* is found in 2 Corinthians 2:11 that says, "Lest
Satan should take advantage of us; for we are not ignorant of his
devices (noema)." We are not ignorant of Satan's darkened mental
perception.

Other uses of noema are found in the following verses. As you read
each verse, replace the word *noema* for the words *mental perception*.

> But their minds (noema) were blinded: for until
> this day remaineth the same vail untaken away in
> the reading of the old testament; which vail is done
> away in Christ. (2 Corinthians 3:14 KJV)

> In whom the god of this world hath blinded the
> minds (noema) of them which believe not, lest
> the light of the glorious gospel of Christ, who is
> the image of God, should shine unto them. (2
> Corinthians 4:4 KJV)

> Casting down imaginations, and every high thing
> that exalteth itself against the knowledge of God,

and bringing into captivity every thought (noema) to the obedience of Christ. (2 Corinthians 10:5 KJV)

And the peace of God, which passeth all understanding, shall keep your hearts and minds (noema) through Christ Jesus. (Philippians 4:7 KJV)

But I fear, lest by any means, as the serpent beguiled Eve through his subtilty, so your minds (noema) should be corrupted from the simplicity that is in Christ. (2 Corinthians 11:3 KJV)

Perception is an interesting thing. We are told that at the scene of a crime or an accident the police officer will take several statements from a number of eye witnesses. However, we have heard it said many times that each witness can have a different perspective of what happened. What's true for one may not be true for another. In fact, these "eyewitnesses" can have completely opposite viewpoints. It all depends on their point of reference, their frame of mind, and their mental state or their way of looking at things. It all comes down to perspective. Our perspective is everything.

In 2 Corinthians 11:3 Paul was talking to believers and warning them not to be deceived as Eve had been so their minds, their perspective would not be corrupted from the simplicity that is in Christ. If something is corrupted, it is damaged. The Bible often uses the word *defiled*. This corruption or defilement came into the mind of man at the fall, and the seed continued to everyone born on this earth. But when a heart is opened to Jesus, then that seed of corruption ceases. When you are born again, you are born of an incorruptible seed that does not die.

> Being born again, not of corruptible seed, but of incorruptible, by the word of God, which liveth and abideth for ever. (1 Peter1:23 KJV)

The way we perceive determines everything. The way we view life, truth, love, ourselves, and God is according to the light that is in us. Jesus explains this in the following verses.

> The light of the body is the eye: if therefore thine eye be single, thy whole body shall be full of light. But if thine eye be evil, thy whole body shall be full of darkness. If therefore the light that is in thee be darkness, how great is that darkness! (Matthew 6:22–23 KJV)

> The lamp of the body is the eye. Therefore, when your eye is good, your whole body also is full of light. But when your eye is bad, your body also is full of darkness. Therefore take heed that the light which is in you is not darkness. If then your whole body is full of light, having no part dark, the whole body will be full of light, as when the bright shining of a lamp gives you light. (Luke 11:34–36 NKJV)

Light brings clarity.

The lamp of the body is the eye. The eye represents our perception. If our eye is single, then our whole body is full of light. This word single is the Greek word *haplous,* and it means simple, in which there is nothing complicated or confusing, without folds, whole, good, fulfilling its office, and clear. It also means singleness of purpose and to have an undivided heart.

This tells us that if our perception is correct, then we will see clearly and know what is true. The right perception brings clarity about God and about life. Jesus is the light of the world and He is the truth. Light and truth cause us to have the right perspective and to see clearly. The correct knowledge of Christ and His finished work causes us to have the right perspective. When we know the truth about how God really sees us, then we see correctly. How well we perceive is how well we receive.

It's interesting to note that even the natural eye can determine the wholeness of the body. Medical science has discovered a connection between healing and the eye. Diagnosing illness through the eye is actually nothing new. Doctors tell us there are dozens of diseases, from high blood pressure to certain cancers and even heart disease that can be detected in the eye.

If your eye is not sound, it affects your whole body. If your perception is not correct, it affects your whole life.

Vine's Expository Dictionary definition of the Greek word for light is phos and states that "light requires an organ to discern form and color. Where light is absent, or where it has become impaired from any cause, it is useless. Man, naturally, is incapable of receiving spiritual light inasmuch as he lacks the capacity for spiritual things. Hence believers are called 'sons of light,' not merely because they have received a revelation from God, but because in the new birth they have received the spiritual capacity for it."[1]

Did you catch that? It takes the light of the gospel that regenerates the spirit of man in order for man to even begin to have the ability to receive spiritual truth.

In John 1:4, the Bible says that in Christ was Life and the Life was the light of men. And the light shines on in the dark, and the darkness has never overpowered it. Verse 9 goes on to say the true Light, Christ, coming into the world and illumines every person. This "light" is defined as the power of understanding. It's the power to comprehend. It's the eternal spirit of man in union with the Holy Spirit. In Proverbs 20:27 we read that the spirit of man is the lamp of the Lord. The Amplified Bible says it this way:

> The spirit of man [that factor in human personality which proceeds immediately from God] is the lamp of the Lord, searching all his innermost parts. (AMPC)

> The breath of man [is] a lamp of Jehovah, Searching all the inner parts of the heart. (YLT)

As the famous hymn "Amazing Grace" declares, "I was lost, but now I'm found. I was blind, but now I see." The glory that covered Adam and Eve gave them the right perspective. They saw clearly. They had the power to understand. Their perception was clear about who they were, about who their Creator was, and about their relationship with each other. They knew that God was well pleased with them!

Truth sees clearly. Truth sees reality. A lie changes the perception. The truth is that as born-again believers, we've been placed into Christ. Our new identity is in Christ. And because we are in Christ, we can see clearly. We see the truth of God's love for us. We know beyond all doubt that God's love for us is never-ending. We understand that God's love toward does not change in spite of any of our shortcomings. He does not change. He is the same today, yesterday, and forever. That is having the right perspective. That is seeing clearly. That is the truth.

GOD IS GOOD

When the Israelites were in bondage in Egypt, God chose Moses to be their leader. That's an amazing thing because unlike the world today, the Bible says God chose the most humble man on the face of the earth to lead more than two million people. But that's God's way. It's no wonder Moses had an extraordinary relationship with the Lord. In Exodus 33 we find God talking with Moses about how to lead the Israelites. Moses says he cannot do it unless God goes with him, and the Lord assures Moses that His presence will go with him.

Then in verse 18 Moses asked the Lord a wonderful question: And he said, "Please, show me Your glory." And God's response was, "I will make all My goodness pass before you, and I will proclaim the name of the Lord before you."

We have to ask ourselves some questions here. Why would Moses ask God to show him His glory? Moses had been in the presence of God many times up to this point. He had talked with God on Mount Sinai numerous times. Moses had seen God's presence in the burning bush, in the cloud by day, and in the fire by night. He had heard God's voice from the burning bush and even spoken with him face to face at his tabernacle. Furthermore, Moses witnessed God's mighty power over and over again as Pharaoh continued to resist the release of the children of Israel. Not to mention the miraculous parting of the Red Sea, the supernatural provision of manna and water gushing forth from a rock! Even after all these incredible displays of God's power, how is it that Moses asks, "Show me Your glory?"

The glory of God is indeed His power, but interestingly, when Moses asked to see His glory, God chose to show Moses His goodness! There's no doubt Moses knew God could do anything. However, I believe the heart of Moses was to really know God, to really know who He was, not just what He could do. The reason I say this is because of what Moses asked God's leading up to this.

> Now therefore, I pray, if I have found grace in Your sight, show me now Your way, that I may know You and that I may find grace in Your sight. (Exodus 33:13 NKJV)

Moses knew who God was by His power, but I believe Moses wanted to know God in another way, to know another aspect of Him, to know His heart. We find that God chose to show Moses who He was by giving him an experience of His goodness. So we come to understand that one aspect of God's glory is His goodness. We come to understand that to know God is to know He is good! By revealing His goodness, God showed Moses who He was. God responded to Moses by saying He was going to have all His goodness pass before him. Wow! Now if we think of all the "power" God has displayed, which is an aspect of His glory, then we can only imagine how tremendous and magnificent His goodness must be! In fact, God's goodness is so magnificent that He told Moses He would only show His backside. Otherwise it would kill him! Not only is it impossible for our natural minds to conceive the magnitude of the goodness of God, but our physical bodies would incinerate in the presence of the goodness of God. That's why our last transformation will be from our earthly body that was made of dust to a glorified body.

So intense is the goodness of God that the Bible says He put Moses in the cleft of a rock, which is symbolic of our placement in Christ, and He also put His hand over Moses as He passed by.

> And he said, "I will make all my goodness pass before you and will proclaim before you my name 'The Lord.' And I will be gracious to whom I will be gracious, and will show mercy on whom I will show mercy. But," he said, "you cannot see my face, for man shall not see me and live." And the Lord said, "Behold, there is a place by me where you shall stand on the rock, and while my glory passes by I will put you in a cleft of the rock, and I will cover you with my hand until I have passed by. Then I will take away my hand, and you shall see my back, but my face shall not be seen." (Exodus 33:19–23 ESV)

INTIMACY

Now after this amazing encounter Moses had with God's goodness, the Lord made a covenant with man by giving the law, namely the Ten Commandments. These were the rules the Israelites were to live by to be in covenant, to be in relationship with God. Of course, God knew they could not keep the law. But man needed to be conscious of the sinfulness of sin, so the law was given so man would realize his inability to keep it. As a result, man would see his need for God's intervention to save him from his sin. The law is perfect, but when man chooses to live life his own way, destruction, pain, sorrow, and death are inevitable. Sin leads to death. It doesn't take a genius to see that the whole earth is steeped in sin and in dire need of a Savior. There is no other solution.

> God's law was given so that all people could see how sinful they were. But as people sinned more and more, God's wonderful grace became more abundant. (Romans 5:20 NLT)

In chapter 34 of Exodus, we read that Moses was on Mount Sinai with the Lord forty days and forty nights without food or water while he wrote on the tablets of stone as the Lord directed him. The most incredible thing about this is that when Moses came down from the mountain, he did not know it, but his face was actually shining and sending out beams of light! The Israelites were so shocked at the sight of Moses that they were afraid to come near him. After being in God's presence and experiencing His goodness, the glory that radiated from Moses was overwhelming! He was literally shining with the glory of God! Moses spoke to the people all the commandments that God had given him, but then he had to put a veil on his face because they could not continually look at him. The glory that radiated from his face was too brilliant! Interestingly though, when Moses went in to talk with the Lord, he took the veil off.

> When Moses came down from Mount Sinai with the two tablets of the covenant law in his hands, he was not aware that his face was radiant because he had spoken with the Lord. When Aaron and all the Israelites saw Moses, his face was radiant, and they were afraid to come near him. But Moses called to them; so Aaron and all the leaders of the community came back to him, and he spoke to them. Afterward all the Israelites came near him, and he gave them all the commands the Lord had given him on Mount Sinai. When Moses finished speaking to them, he put a veil over his face. But whenever he entered the Lord's presence to speak with him, he removed the veil until he came out. And when he came out and told the Israelites what he had been commanded, they saw that his face was radiant. Then Moses would put the veil back over his face until he went in to speak with the Lord. (Exodus 34:29–35 NIV)

Now God's ultimate purpose has not changed. He created man to be in a close and personal relationship with Him. But that relationship must be based on love and trust, not on our ability to follow a set of rules. Since the commandments could never be fully obeyed, they set men up to failure. It was impossible for man to ever have a perfect relationship with God through the law. The Bible says the law was written on tablets of stone. They were hard. They were cold and rigid. There is nothing personal about following a set of rules. The law does not bring man into the intimate relationship that God desires. Furthermore, man's inability to keep the law because of his sin nature continually produces death in his life.

> The old way, with laws etched in stone, led to death.
> (2 Corinthians 3:7 NLT)

God is concerned with the heart of man. Our relationship with Him can never be based on our performance to do all the right things. Whenever we attempt to present ourselves before God in that way, we are simply trying to be acceptable to Him in our own efforts. The Bible calls this works of the flesh. Works of the flesh will never constitute a right relationship between God and man. Unfortunately, man has the propensity to slip back into a "works" mentality to feel acceptable to God. Now with that in mind, consider the Israelites. The glory of God on the face of Moses was God's presence. However, the glory had to be covered because the people could not withstand coming into God's presence without having a sense of fear. They were fearful before God and they did not feel accepted. The reason for this is because the old covenant, the Old Testament, is based on following the law, which we know can never be met. We understand that this veil created a separation between man and God.

Consider this in light of the fall of man. We know Adam and Eve made their own choice in the garden rather than following God's instruction. We also know that when this happened, their relationship with God changed so much so that they became afraid and hid from His presence. Their perspective about the relationship they had always known and experienced with Him changed. They did not believe they were accepted and welcomed in God's presence. They were afraid to face God. They were afraid He didn't love them anymore.

Again, God's ultimate concern is the heart of man and the restoration of an intimate relationship. However, a veil still covers people's hearts when they try to come before God through their own efforts. There can never be any freedom to come before God in this way. That is because the perspective is all wrong!

> But their minds were blinded. For until this day the same veil remains unlifted in the reading of the Old Testament, because the veil is taken away in Christ. But even to this day, when Moses is read, a veil lies on their heart. (2 Corinthians 3:14–15 NKJV)

The Greek word for blinded in this verse is *poroo*, and it means to harden or make dull or to lose the power of understanding. Trying to have a relationship with God by following the law, following a set of rules, is completely impersonal. God wants a personal relationship with us, so trying to approach Him by our performance actually dulls our hearts to discover the true nature of God because we are focused on what we should do to try to measure up to Him. Remember, we could never do enough to measure up to God's standard, which is perfection. When we attempt to approach God in this way, we are blinded, or we can say we have lost the power to understand or perceive. Our perspective is wrong. That's why the veil or we can say the blindness is taken away when we receive all Christ did for us.

In Christ Jesus the veil has been rent! We must understand that it is not what we do for God that matters but only what has been done by Christ. When we turn to Him and see the truth, the veil is lifted, and our perspective becomes clear. We see the truth that God loves and accepts us completely. We come freely with open faces before God with no sense of fear because we know God now sees us in the perfection of His Son, and we see ourselves in the perfection of His Son! This is when true and lasting transformation takes place.

> Nevertheless when one turns to the Lord, the veil is taken away. Now the Lord is the Spirit; and where the Spirit of the Lord is, there is liberty. But we all, with unveiled face, beholding as in a mirror the glory of the Lord, are being transformed into the same image from glory to glory, just as by the Spirit of the Lord. (2 Corinthians 3:16–18 NKJV)

We have been placed into the new covenant, the new agreement between God and man through the precious blood of Christ. And it is not a set of laws written on hard stone tablets, but it is the Holy Spirit within who speaks to our hearts. It is an inner witness of the Holy Spirit, who is the Spirit of Truth, leading and guiding our lives. Of course the Holy Spirit is in full agreement with God and His word, so ultimately we are following the law, but it is because we our being led in our hearts through a personal relationship with our Creator. It is a Spirit-to-spirit, heart-to-heart relationship. It is intimate. It is holy. It is a personal union and communion that we are blessed to experience and enjoy with our heavenly Father. It is the loving relationship between God and man established through Christ.

> This is a covenant not of written laws, but of the Spirit. The old written covenant ends in death; but under the new covenant, the Spirit gives life. (2 Corinthians 3:6 NLT)

When Jesus hung on the cross, His last words spoken before He died were, "It is finished!" At that very moment, the veil that separated the holy place from the holy of holies in the Jewish tabernacle was torn in half from top to bottom. This veil or curtain was said to be sixty feet high, thirty feet wide, and four inches thick. There is no question that God Himself tore the veil. It represents the separation between man and his accessibility to God. This veil represents the separation that is stripped away when we receive Christ. It is a cutting away of the flesh of the heart, a cutting away of our trying to perform to be acceptable to God. That's why it is freedom. That's why it is liberty that can only be found in Christ. He and He alone made it possible for us to come back into an intimate relationship with our Creator, our Father God! Jesus did it all! So with unveiled faces we come right into the very presence of God without any thought of fear. There is no more striving. We can rest in the finished work of Christ, knowing we are accepted and approved and welcomed into the presence of God! And beholding as in a mirror the glory of the Lord, we are changed into the same image from glory to glory! We receive what God says in His word to us that we are His beloved children in whom He is well pleased, as if we were looking into a mirror. We receive the truth that we are a new creation in Christ. As we receive the glory of the Lord, His good opinion of us, then we are changed into His very same image, from glory to glory. We begin to reflect His glory. We are changed from honor and majesty to more honor and majesty.

We find in the book of Jeremiah the Lord speaking to the prophet about the new covenant He will establish in the days ahead.

> "The day is coming," says the Lord, "when I will make a new covenant with the people of Israel and Judah. This covenant will not be like the one I made with their ancestors when I took them by the hand and brought them out of the land of Egypt. They broke that covenant, though I loved them as a husband loves his wife," says the Lord. "But this

is the new covenant I will make with the people of Israel after those days," says the Lord. "I will put my instructions deep within them, and I will write them on their hearts. I will be their God, and they will be my people. And they will not need to teach their neighbors, nor will they need to teach their relatives, saying, 'You should know the Lord.' For everyone, from the least to the greatest, will know me already," says the Lord. "And I will forgive their wickedness, and I will never again remember their sins." (Jeremiah 31:31–34 NLT)

God is amazingly good!

GOD IS LOVE

~ *m* ~

G od is love. And because God is love, love is the greatest force
in life and in the entire universe. For us to live without God's
love or to even feel unloved by God to any degree is a great hindrance
to our lives. It limits us in all that God has destined and planned
for us to do. Every person born has a need and desire to be loved
and valued. Ultimately, that place of need is reserved for and can
only be filled with God, who is love. Until that place in our hearts
is filled with the love of God, there is lack inside, and there is
a searching for something to fill that void. This truth is seen in
every culture throughout the world. People look to be satisfied in
a number of ways. Sometimes it's through relationships, sometimes
in the pursuit of money, and for some it can be their career, or some
type of religion. Oftentimes people try to find fulfillment through
some type of entertainment or anything else that will bring a sense
of completeness. Love from our family and friends is probably the
most satisfying to the majority of people and does bring a level of
wholeness to our lives. However, nothing can or ever will bring the
fullness of acceptance, approval, and identity to our lives like the
love of God our Creator can bring and will bring. He is love. He is
pure love. He is perfect love.

When people do not know the love of God, they often try to
establish a sense of worth or value to their lives through others.
Jesus recognized this truth with the religious leaders of His day. In

John 5 we find Jesus being persecuted because He healed a man on the Sabbath. According to Jewish tradition, it was not lawful to heal on the Sabbath. He responded by saying that the Father is always working and that He also must be working. I love that Jesus calls healing people, setting them free, providing their needs, and loving them, work. These works are God's deeds and His acts. It's what God does because that's His nature.

Jesus goes on to explain that He does not act independently, but He only does what He sees the Father do, as we have already established. The decisions and judgments He makes are right because He does not seek His will but only the will of the Father. He continues by telling the religious leaders that He does not testify concerning Himself, but there is another who testifies of Him. This is a direct reference to the Father's declaration, "This is My Beloved Son in Whom I am well pleased!" The audible voice that was heard at the baptism of Jesus and on the Mount of Transfiguration was God's testimony of His Son, as I have already confirmed through the word. Jesus said that if He testified in His own behalf, then His testimony would not be valid, and it would not be worth anything.

> "I can do nothing on my own. As I hear, I judge, and my judgment is just, because I seek not my own will but the will of him who sent me. If I alone bear witness about myself, my testimony is not true. There is another who bears witness about me, and I know that the testimony that he bears about me is true." (John 5:30–32 ESV)

> If I alone testify in My behalf, My testimony is not valid and cannot be worth anything. There is Another Who testifies concerning Me, and I know and am certain that His evidence on My behalf is true and valid. (John 5:31–32 AMPC)

He continues by explaining that not only did God's words testify of Him, but the very works that He displayed were a witness that God sent Him. It's a curious thing to think that Jesus did miracle after miracle right before their eyes, yet the people refused to acknowledge Him as the Son of God. These men were supposed to be the religious leaders who knew scripture, yet the very scriptures testified of Christ. These men were constantly challenging His authority, confronting His every action, dishonoring His character, and even plotting to kill Him. They refused to hear what Jesus had to say. Their hearts were closed to the very person who had the words of life. They shut their hearts to God's message and to God's messenger.

Then Jesus makes an eye-opening statement!

> He says, "I know you and recognize and understand that you have not the love of God in you." (John 5:42 AMPC)

There's a wonderful revelation in this statement.

These men took pride in their religious status. They viewed themselves as superior to the common people. They took pleasure in giving and receiving accolades from one another. They were self-righteous. They were hypocritical. They loved being the center of attention as they praised and honored each other. That's why Jesus said they did not have God's love. Their sense of importance, their sense of value and worth came from each other! These religious leaders did not know God. They did not know that God loved them. Jesus had the words of the Father for them, but they shut their ears to His message.

> How is it possible for you to believe [how can you learn to believe], you who [are content to seek and] receive praise and honor and glory from one another,

and yet do not seek the praise and honor and glory which come from Him Who alone is God? (John 5:44 AMPC)

It's the love of God that truly changes a heart. It's the love of God that brings true fulfillment. It's the love of our Creator that gives true meaning, purpose, and value to our lives. Remember, Jesus said, "My honor *must* come to me from My Father." Now our honor *must* come to us from our Father God. There is no other source.

God's love is a strength that is more powerful than we can imagine. Love has to give. That is what it does. It is a force that gives out to others. It is not a withholder. Love gives. Since God is love, it is God's nature to give. For God to withhold love would mean for Him to go against the essence of who He is. John 3:16 reminds us of this. For God so loved the world that He gave His only begotten Son that whosoever believes on Him should not perish, but have everlasting life. Love gave His very best. God gave His very best. He gave His most precious treasure and the closest thing to His heart.

Romans 8 tells us there is now no condemnation for those who are in Christ Jesus, for the law of the Spirit of Life in Christ has set us free from the law of sin and death. We are no longer held in bondage to death. We are no longer held in bondage to fear, which is an aspect of death. Remember when Adam and Eve disobeyed God by eating the fruit in the garden, the first thing they experienced was fear because they hid. Adam said he was afraid so he hid because he was naked. The glory had left him. The knowledge of his right standing with God had left him. The knowledge of his complete acceptance and approval with his Father left him so fear came in because fear brings the thought of punishment. Adam did not know if God loved him.

It is one thing to say that you believe that God exists but quite another thing to say God exists and I know Him and I know that

He loves me. Sad to say, there are people who have received Christ as Lord and Savior, but they're not sure if He loves them. They feel no security when faced with difficult situations in life. They begin to worry, have doubts, and eventually become fearful. Today people are fearful of so many things. They fear the unknown. They fear death, lack, sickness, or not having their needs met. People are afraid of flying, afraid of snakes, afraid of the dark, afraid of storms, and the list goes on and on. There's no peace when you go through life fearful of so many things. The Bible says perfect love casts out fear. Fear brings the thought of punishment or you could say the thought of pain. Being afraid causes a person to think something could happen to bring some type of harm to them. But God's love casts out fear. There's no fear in love. God is love, and perfect love casts out fear. So in our union with Christ, we experience God's perfect love, and all fears vanish. We can live in absolute security no matter what the situation might be.

It is vital for us to receive the love that only God can give in order for us to enjoy and experience life to the fullness God intended. We must come to the place where we know we are completely, absolutely, unconditionally loved by our Creator every moment of every day one hundred percent of the time. And the good news is that it is possible!

The love of our Father God is enough to enable us to walk through any situation in this life. The Bible says that eternal life is to know God. Since that's a true statement, then we can say eternal life is to know love. Again, the love of God is the most powerful force there is. We must come to the place where we know, that we know, that we know we are unconditionally loved, approved of, and accepted by our heavenly Father today, tomorrow, and forever. We were created to know this truth. It is the truth that sets us free.

WE'VE BEEN HONORED AND GLORIFIED

When I consider Your heavens, the work of Your fingers, The moon and the stars, which You have ordained, What is man that You are mindful of him, And the son of man that You visit him? (Psalm 8:3–4 NKJV)

This is absolutely an overwhelming picture of the heart of love that our heavenly Father God and our Lord and Savior Jesus Christ has for mankind. The passion that God has to enjoy an intimate relationship with man could not be expressed in a more profound way. This passage in Psalms was written by King David. I can just picture David tending the sheep late at night, lying out in the fields, and looking up into the beautiful, starry sky. Considering the immensity, the majesty, and the awesomeness of His Creator as revealed through His creation, he had to ask, "Who am I? Who is man that You would visit him? Who is man that You would come down to save him?" The mind and heart of this infinite being was focused on His love for mankind. David knew it, and it overwhelmed him. He continued with this revelation by saying;

> For You have made him a little lower than the angels, And You have crowned him with glory and honor. You have made him to have dominion over

the works of Your hands; You have put all things
under his feet, All sheep and oxen—Even the beasts
of the field, The birds of the air, And the fish of
the sea That pass through the paths of the seas. O
Lord, our Lord, How excellent is Your name in all
the earth! (Psalm 8:5-9 NKJV)

David is making a direct reference to creation in
Genesis 1:26–28:

Then God said, "Let Us make man in Our image,
according to Our likeness; let them have dominion
over the fish of the sea, over the birds of the air,
and over the cattle, over all the earth and over every
creeping thing that creeps on the earth." So God
created man in His own image; in the image of
God He created him; male and female He created
them. Then God blessed them, and God said to
them, "Be fruitful and multiply; fill the earth and
subdue it; have dominion over the fish of the sea,
over the birds of the air, and over every living thing
that moves on the earth." (NKJV)

We see that from David's reference in Psalms that man was created
in God's image, made a little lower than the angels, crowned with
honor and glory (as I have talked about extensively), and given
dominion over every fish, bird, animal, and insect. Not only that,
but in Genesis 2:15 God said to take care of the earth. Adam and Eve
were commanded to bear children, multiply this beautiful earth, and
have authority over it. This was God's gift to man. We were created
to enjoy life abundantly in His perfect creation.

Now we know Adam forfeited the glory he once had because
of deception. But God, in His great mercy, has reconciled us to

Himself. By placing us into Christ, we've been lifted up to a position of dignity. We are in the King of Kings. We've been crowned with glory and honor. We've been put into royalty. It's a high standing, the highest standing by virtue of being in Christ. We are sons and daughters of God Almighty, Creator of heaven and earth. He has bestowed glory and honor upon us. We have been placed into a royal position. God says, "Royalty becomes you! Royalty suits you! Royalty looks good on you!"

The mystery is Christ within, the hope of glory, the hope of realizing the glory within. It's a positive expectation of glory within. It's already within. Everything that Christ accomplished for us is already on the inside. The kingdom of God is within. Every need is already there. God said He's already given us everything that pertains to life and godliness. It's all within because it is Christ Himself within. In the kingdom, there is no shortage. There's no lack. Nothing is being withheld. It's all been provided, and it's all available. We already have our inheritance. Christ is our inheritance. That is why we can rest!

The apostle Paul recites a prayer in the first chapter of Ephesians that I believe clearly expresses the truth that as believers we have been glorified and honored by the Father. In this prayer, Paul asks God for three things. First and foremost, he asks that we would have the correct knowledge and understanding of who God really is. Then *from that truth, from that accurate perspective of the Father,* our eyes would be opened to see the glorious person He created us to be in Christ, the glorious person Christ is in us, and the understanding that the same power that raised Christ from the dead is available because we believe!

> That the God of our Lord Jesus Christ, the Father of glory, may give you the Spirit of wisdom and of revelation in the knowledge of him, having the eyes of your hearts enlightened, that you may know what

> is the hope to which he has called you, what are the
> riches of his glorious inheritance in the saints, and
> what is the immeasurable greatness of his power
> toward us who believe, according to the working of
> his great might that he worked in Christ when he
> raised him from the dead and seated him at his right
> hand in the heavenly places. (Ephesians 1:17–20)

God has overwhelmed us with majesty. Honor, glory, and dignity have been bestowed upon us because we are in Christ Jesus, who is the name above every name, who is exalted high above! When this truth becomes a revelation and a reality, then our perspective will change. We know where we are, who we are, and whose we are. Our outlook on life and all its circumstances begins to change. Having a kingly mind-set changes everything. It changes our whole perspective of how we see ourselves and how we see others. We adjust to the light within. We adjust to the truth within. As believers, we are recreated in Christ Jesus, reconciled to our Father, and placed into a heavenly dignity as sons and daughters of the Most High! We are in the royal family. Because we are seated with the King of Kings in majesty, we have a different perspective about what happens on earth. We are high above, secure, with all things available to us. We honor our Father, Christ, and the Holy Spirit by abiding in this place Jesus purchased for us. In this position, we have all rank, rights, and privileges of heaven. We are sons and daughters of the Most High God. He has made us accepted in His Beloved Son. It is our true identity.

> Blessed be the God and Father of our Lord Jesus
> Christ, who has blessed us with every spiritual
> blessing in the heavenly places in Christ, just as He
> chose us in Him before the foundation of the world,
> that we should be holy and without blame before
> Him in love, having predestined us to adoption as

sons by Jesus Christ to Himself, according to the
good pleasure of His will, to the praise of the glory
of His grace, by which He made us accepted in the
Beloved. (Ephesians 1:3–6 NKJV)

Open your heart and receive the all honor and glory that only your
heavenly Father can give. It is His heart's desire for you.

And those whom He thus foreordained, He also
called; and those whom He called, He also justified
(acquitted, made righteous, putting them into
right standing with Himself). And those whom
He justified, He also glorified [raising them to a
heavenly dignity and condition or state of being].
(Romans 8:30 AMPC)

God loves us so much that He put us into His Beloved Son, and He
declares boldly, *"You are my sons and daughters, in whom I am well
pleased!"*

Endnotes

1   Vine, E.W., Unger, Merrill F., White, William Jr., *Vines Complete
Expository Dictionary of Old and New Testament Words* (Thomas Nelson,
Inc., Nashville, TN, 1984)

Printed in the United States
By Bookmasters